THE EXTRA MILE

10

Century
20 Vauxhall Bridge Road
London SW1V 2SA

Century is part of the Penguin Random House group of companies
whose addresses can be found at global.penguinrandomhouse.com

First published by Century in 2023

www.penguin.co.uk

A CIP catalogue record for this book is available from the British Library.

ISBN 9781529903058

Typeset in 13.25/17.5pt Goudy Oldstyle Std by Jouve (UK), Milton Keynes
Printed and bound in Great Britain by Clays Ltd, Elcograf S.p.A.

The authorised representative in the EEA is Penguin Random House Ireland,
Morrison Chambers, 32 Nassau Street, Dublin D02 YH68

www.greenpenguin.co.uk

Penguin Random House is committed to a sustainable future for
our business, our readers and our planet. This book is made
from Forest Stewardship Council® certified paper.

THE EXTRA MILE
KEVIN SINFIELD

WITH PAUL HAYWARD

To Jayne, Jack and Sam

CONTENTS

FOREWORD BY ROB BURROW

What do you say about a man like Kevin who has already achieved so much in his life?

Where do I start? The *BBC Breakfast* TV show has often asked me to write something about Kevin, but to be honest I run out of words to describe him. Seeing as this is his autobiography, I'll do my best here.

Ever since we first met as youngsters in Leeds before we turned pro, Kevin has always been a great friend to me. People who don't know the real Kevin see that he has this burning sense of purpose, this inner hope and drive to make the impossible possible. That's true. His incredible endurance fund-raisers for MND (motor neurone disease) over the last few years have shown everyone his spirit – more on these challenges in a moment. But having shared a dressing room at Leeds Rhinos for nearly fifteen years with Kevin, I want briefly to share a few things that you might not know about him, or that might surprise you, before you start reading his book.

First up, the man smells fantastic. Kevin was always a

very well-presented guy as a player. It got to the point where I once even bought the same moisturiser as him so that I could have the same smell whenever I breezed into the changing rooms (as he would do).

Kevin was also the fashion icon and trend-setter in the team. He was the first player at Rhinos to wear leggings without shorts. Our team-mate Adrian Morley could never wrap his head around that one at England camps, but despite the fashion risk and the teasing, the look caught on, and many of us, myself included, would eventually follow suit.

In fact, Kevin was always so immaculately turned out and well dressed that it got to the point where the lads thought he was obsessive, or a bit too fond of himself. But jokes aside, this couldn't be further from the truth. Kevin's obsessiveness, like everything he does, ultimately helps other people, in conscious and unconscious ways. Whether it's the 'performance' benefits of leggings in training, or a bit more self-care and pride in your appearance when playing, Kevin has always been an example that helps bring people together. But he also likes looking good . . .

In our playing days, Kevin was the ultimate captain who led from the front. Cool, calm and collected. In the team, we all wanted to stay close to him. He once said that you become the average of the five people you hang around with. We all wanted to be around Kevin and be the professional he was.

In more recent years, Kevin was there for me on day one of my MND diagnosis, and he has stayed alongside me ever since, every step of the way. My mate has won so many accolades in his career but no one expected him to do so much for a disease few people knew much about. Throughout the challenges, from the build-up to the finishing line, he has kept me emotionally involved with each and every event, whether it's the ridiculous amount of planning that's involved or the extraordinary amount of stress that he puts on his body – especially the pain he endured throughout his second challenge, the Extra Mile, when he ran 101 miles in twenty-four hours. I think my daughter Macy was looking for a race when she ran alongside Kevin in the final stretch of the challenge to enter Headingley stadium, but I think Kevin was in survival mode by that point, bless him.

I'm lost for words when I think of Kevin, because what can you say about someone who has made such an impact on so many lives in a lifetime, both in his career and throughout the fund-raisers? How was he able to get so many people, during a cost-of-living crisis, to give so much money to MND? It just shows the amount of love the public have for the main man Kev.

I won't go on much longer – Kevin is always to the point, and I know this will embarrass him. But to finish, I have to say one final thing about the man himself and the fund-raisers he has taken on for me since my diagnosis. What sort of friend would put his life at risk for me, forgoing sleep, spending time apart from his family and risking permanent injury or worse? I've said this many times, but the world would be a better place with more people like Sir Kev in it.

I hope by reading this book some of Kevin's magic, some of his leadership and some of his big-heartedness will rub off on you. You might even smell better too.

INTRODUCTION

One wintry afternoon in November 2022 I ran through the gates of Headingley to see a familiar figure waiting for me by the statue of John Holmes, a Leeds rugby league legend. Rob Burrow sat in his wheelchair, with sunglasses on, his wife Lindsey by his side, as the crowd clamoured for photos of him. Just above Rob's head was an inscription on the John Holmes statue: 'The Reluctant Hero'.

Rob wouldn't have wanted to be sitting there in the cold, quietly, unable to move much as a result of the motor neurone disease (MND) he was diagnosed with in December 2019. And ordinarily I wouldn't have been running seven back-to-back ultra-marathons in the last week of a Rugby League World Cup staged in England. But there we were at Headingley, me and the reluctant hero, united in the fight against MND, just as we'd battled together in many great Leeds Rhinos teams.

I'd passed through those gates as a thirteen-year-old from Oldham having crossed the Pennines with my mum and dad to see whether Leeds might be the club for me. Now I was forty-two, running ultra no. 6. The ground where I'd played for twenty years rose in front of me once again.

My boyhood years on the Leeds training ground had brought me into contact with a younger, tiny, firefly game-changer who would become my team-mate and friend during the club's finest trophy-winning years. There he was again, this time in a wheelchair, silently absorbing the love of the crowd.

We slowed to a jog and then a walk as TV cameras and support staff closed in on me and our Ultra 7 in 7 team of runners and cyclists. Normally I would stop to catch my breath and talk on live TV, but this time I kept walking through the throng, towards Rob, with a smile on my face. There was an even bigger one on his, despite what MND was doing to his body.

With the crowd held back, I lowered my head to Rob's. Lindsey threw a bench coat over me to keep me warm but it slipped over my head to form a kind of cocoon for me and Rob. I thanked him for coming, apologised for being so sweaty, and told him: 'I love you, pal, all right?'

No words came back.

I straightened myself to speak to the large gathering and managed a couple of sentences about how wonderful it was to be there, but couldn't go on. Standing to the side of Rob's chair, I dropped my head, bent over, clasped my knees with my hands and tried to compose myself to resume my speech. There was a hush. Nothing moved or made a sound while I gathered myself to carry on. Looking straight ahead, Rob couldn't have known why this silence had descended; why I was lost for words.

From the crowd came a lone shout of encouragement, then the rising sound of clapping.

I let go of my knees, lifted my head and straightened back up. The words rose in me too. Carrying on was what this was all about. Now I was standing upright again and talking to the crowd in the Headingley car park, paying tribute to Rob's courage, telling them why we were doing this, and how people all along the route had come out to share their stories and seek strength from the campaign we were all part of.

Somehow, the men we used to be on that Headingley pitch had become the men standing beside that statue, surrounded by kindness and empathy. The fans who had cheered us so many times on cold winter nights were now supporting us in a greater cause. It felt like a rugby league event – the Leeds Rhinos mascot was out there, geeing up the crowd – but there was no mistaking how much our lives had changed since the club's golden run of Grand Final and Challenge Cup wins.

The Ultra 7 in 7 ran from 13 to 19 November 2022. It was kicked off by Doddie Weir of Scotland and the British and Irish Lions, who was diagnosed with MND in 2016. Doddie, who had been Rob's guide and mentor when Rob was first diagnosed, joined us on the start line at Murrayfield at 7 a.m.

3

on a cold and dark Scottish morning. Later that day he was wheeled on to the Murrayfield pitch by his three sons, Hamish, Angus and Ben, ahead of the Scotland v. New Zealand autumn international. Both teams walked across the pitch and surrounded him to applaud his bravery. The crowd gave him a rousing ovation. You couldn't have scripted a more emotional reception for a great Scottish hero.

As we headed south on our ultras through Doddie's Borders heartland and into England, our aim was to connect the stories of Rob, Doddie, Stephen Darby and Ed Slater – all MND sufferers in sport – to the whole MND community. The mission of course was to raise funds for MND care and help drive the search for a cure.

We finished on the pitch at Old Trafford at half-time in the Rugby League World Cup final between Australia and Samoa – another intensely emotional occasion that I will relive in detail later in the story. Seven days after that, our Ultra 7 in 7 team were still swapping memories on our WhatsApp group – and I was still nursing a sore Achilles – when devastating news reached me.

Doddie Weir had died, aged fifty-two, just thirteen days after sending us on our way at Murrayfield. His wife Kathy and sons issued a statement: 'Doddie was an inspirational force of nature. His unending energy and drive, and his strength of character powered him through his rugby and business careers and, we believe, enabled him to fight the effects of Motor Neurone Disease for so many years.'

I added some words of my own: 'I am honoured to have been able to call Doddie my friend and I know his spirit lives on in all of us who knew him. He will always be a champion.'

* * *

This book is the story of my life: my roots in Oldham, my early fascination with captaincy and leadership, the eternal team we forged at Leeds Rhinos, my spell in rugby union at Leeds Carnegie, my time on the office staff of the Rhinos and the Rugby Football League, and my move to become defence coach in union at Leicester Tigers, where I learned so much, made new friends and was able to help bring the rugby codes together around MND. Prominent throughout my story are my beloved family – my wife Jayne, sons Jack and Sam, parents Ray and Beryl, brother Ian and sister Stephanie.

A month after the Ultra 7 in 7, my life took another turn, on a day when both halves of my life converged. On Monday 19 December, I set off in the car to Melrose for Doddie's memorial service. The journey took me past Carlisle, where Doddie and Rob had first met to join forces against MND. It took me through my memory bank of the seven ultra-marathons, which had flowed south from Doddie's heartland. It was a day of intense nostalgia – but one that also opened a new horizon to me.

5

Three hundred and eighty miles to the south on the same day, Steve Borthwick was unveiled as the new England rugby union head coach, replacing Eddie Jones. And I was confirmed by the Rugby Football Union as Steve's defence coach. Steve and I moved from Leicester to England six weeks before the 2023 Six Nations Championship and nine months prior to the World Cup in France.

All sporting lives are divided into two: the playing, and whatever follows. Often the two halves bear little relation. In my case there's a bridge between the two. I've been an administrator and a coach. But Rob's MND caused me to double back to my Leeds Rhinos years and the friendships I made for life there; and to be part of a new team, with a new opponent – MND, which took Doddie so soon after we had run to his former clubs in Melrose and Newcastle.

In this book I set out the things I learned in rugby and in life and how I put them to use in the fight against MND. I hope to give rugby fans a sense of the great games I played in and the wonderful players I shared a pitch with. The bedrock of my life – my family and friends – are influential throughout my story and are given the prominence they deserve.

I'd like to think I've let the reader in on the thrill of playing top-level sport, and I've tried to explain how teams really work. My interest in leadership and how to get the best out of people in your team is a constant theme in these pages. In spirit, the best teams last for ever. I hope you can see that in my accounts of how our Leeds Rhinos sides were so successful.

From the three endurance challenges we've taken on (there may be more to come), we feel two advances have been made, beyond the £7.5 million raised.

First, people are more willing to go to their GP and say: 'I think I've got what Rob Burrow's got.'

Second, and even more powerfully, people who've been diagnosed with MND have long been ashamed to leave the house because they think people won't understand or know what it is. Now, people who are challenged with MND will go out and about and aren't afraid to tell others. The families feel more empowered to say: 'He or she has what Rob Burrow has.'

The front door may be shut. You may be stuck watching daytime TV. But you still have a life. You're still alive. For every single person diagnosed with MND we've got to make it the best journey it can possibly be. If that's about making wider society understand the illness better, Rob has made a huge contribution to finding a way forward for those who will come after him.

For me, it's been a new world of learning; a chance to make use of everything I learned from rugby; an opportunity to be part of a new team, rising from the foundations of the old. In York after day 5 of the Ultra 7 in 7, I searched for the words to explain it: 'If you're doing something for someone else, it's far greater than doing something for yourself.'

I stepped into 2023 with a wonderful new job with the England rugby union team. And I remained determined never to walk away from helping people who need it. The momentum we've built is precious to me and will be a motivation for me for life.

These were our first three challenges:

2020: The Seven in Seven – seven marathons in seven days, each of them under four hours. Monies raised for Rob Burrow's family and £2.2 million to support the MND Association.

2021: The Extra Mile – 101 miles in twenty-four hours, from Leicester to Leeds. £2.5 million raised for the MND Association and Leeds Hospitals Charity appeal for the Rob Burrow Centre for MND. TV viewing figure on BBC *Breakfast* at the finish line at Headingley – 2.3 million.

2022: The Ultra 7 in 7 – seven ultra-marathons in seven days, from Murrayfield to Old Trafford, £2.7 million raised.

It won't stop there.

Kevin Sinfield, January 2023

1

A BRILLIANT MISTAKE

I'm seven years old, standing outside our brown garage door at the bottom of Honey Hill in Saddleworth, waiting to be picked up and taken to the place where it will all begin. I'm in hand-me-downs. I don't have any boots.

My dad is working that morning so we're collected and taken along to a muddy field where I position myself right next to Ian, my older brother, who promptly runs off to play with the under-10s.

I'm left standing alone. And I burst into tears.

The coaches of Waterhead Rugby League Club on the outskirts of Oldham weren't blind to how daunting it was for kids to step into this world for the first time. They knew how to shift a lad quickly from feeling overwhelmed to being in his element.

Straight away, out came the big tackle bags, and we hit them, and dived around in the mud.

I thought: how good's this? Loved it, from that moment on.

The pitches of my youth look very different now: there's actually grass on them. Back then they were fields of mud. I'm a clean and tidy sort by nature but I had no reservations about wallowing in the muck if that was where the contest had to be.

But I was ill equipped for a life in rugby.

Ours was a three-bedroom house, just off South Hill. My parents, who bought it new in the late 1970s, slept bottom left, downstairs. My sister Stephanie and Ian were their only children when they moved in. I was a mistake – conceived, I believe, on the settee one Christmas. They've admitted that. It's always made me laugh. I remind them of this, tell them regularly – I was the best mistake you ever made. My mum and dad had never really wanted three kids. It was simply that they hadn't budgeted for a third child.

In that environment of stretching a week's money as far as it would go, to go and buy a pair of boots for something you might try once or twice – well, it wasn't going to happen. My first pair of boots were handed down from Ian's best mate at school – the old style of rugby boots, Mitre Dragon, with steel toecaps. They were about three sizes too big so I needed a couple of pairs of socks to keep them on.

At the age I first found rugby I never went without, but, as with most working-class families, it was never the posh brands, the smart logos. Not that it bothered me. My life history certainly isn't rags to riches because as I said I didn't go without, but a lot of what I had was passed down from my brother.

Standing here now by that garage door, thinking about where that first ride to Waterhead took me, and the tears on the training pitch, is, well, surreal. I'd have snapped your hand off for how it turned out. Less so for the medals and the trophies than the memories and the experiences: the time people spent helping and supporting me, all that time playing at Leeds, the people I ran on the field with, the friends I have – the unbelievable friends.

Most days I speak to Jamie Jones-Buchanan, my great mate, who I'll refer to as Jamie Jones from here on. We set out on the same path when we signed for Leeds – divergent paths, as it turned out, but it's as strong a friendship as you could have. I'd do anything for him and he'd do anything for me. The same with Rob Burrow. I wasn't as close to Rob as I was to Jamie. But it's the same secure knowledge that you'd give everything for each other.

In the house near the mill where we would go to kick a ball about, Ian and I fought a lot. In fact I got beaten up a lot. The usual brother stuff set off the disputes. In other words, absolutely nothing. Brothers being brothers. Ian was three and a half years older than me. I can remember the day it stopped. There was a radiator next to my bed, and I can recall my head being run along it and making that drumming sound. A decent grounding, you might say, for rugby league.

Ian played semi-pro all the way through. And internationally for Scotland, through our grandad. The underlying message from Ian when we were kids seemed to be: he's my brother, so I can beat him up, but nobody else can. So beyond our family world he was protective, especially when we went to high school. That was handy.

Stephanie went off to Hull University to study geography when I was thirteen. During my childhood she stayed out of the way of my fights with Ian. When Ian was out I'd be stuck at home on my own, and would barge into Steph's room to join her and her friends. I was an absolute nuisance. She's a strong feminist and growing up I respected that. She would always come and watch us play, even though she wasn't fanatical about rugby league. Really supportive.

Family holidays stand out. My dad would spend all his time with the three of us, in the pool, or kicking a football. They saved every penny they had to give us two weeks away. They probably just wanted to lie on a sunbed but there was no chance of that with three kids to entertain. We did five years on the bounce going to Turkey, partly because it was affordable. Spain and Portugal were other escapes. One year we hired a villa and I can remember my mum getting through the best part of a bottle of Bacardi while my dad played with us in the pool. I remind her of that from time to time and she laughs. She wasn't much of a drinker.

You wouldn't guess, but I was mischievous and cheeky, taking great delight in chucking buckets of water over my dad while he was asleep by the pool. It was my way of saying – come on, you've had enough time sleeping, get in the pool. Whenever he was home from work, Dad would be in the back yard kicking a football with me or Ian.

It seems small now, our old house, and overgrown. I hadn't been there for ages until I returned while writing this book. To the left of us is the mill where I played football right the way through. In high school I enjoyed football more than playing for the rugby team.

We weren't very good. But our football team beat Manchester Grammar one year on penalties. I don't know how. It was rainy, muddy, a bog of a pitch, so it suited us more than them. But there were never any offers to me to join a football club. Because I signed professionally at Leeds Rhinos at thirteen, that pretty much mapped things out.

I didn't get in trouble. I was a bit of a pleaser. Probably Ian was a bit more troublesome than I was. But I don't think any one of us was a bad kid. I wanted to be good at things and earn praise. So I did all right at school. Got my GCSEs – A-star, five As, three Bs. My school mates ended up in a range of jobs. Quite a few are teachers, another runs a warehouse, and I have one who runs a socks and undies stall on Oldham market. He started working there when we were fourteen and ended up taking over the business. He's done well with it. Some of my other friends are labourers.

Socially I did all the same things as my contemporaries – but I never drank. Always went out with my mates on a Friday and Saturday but didn't consume alcohol. Never went anywhere near it. I was quite happy in my own skin. My friends respected it. There was never the peer pressure of: go on, you need to get it down you. It helped that I'd signed forms at Leeds at such a young age. They knew what that meant and could see where my priorities were.

I never felt I needed a drink. At the end of the season, as I grew older, I would have one or two, but not many. At first at Leeds my refusal to drink might have counted against me. Lads at that time were still going out for beers a couple of times a week. But I wouldn't. Apart from the first few times when you'd get a hard time from the senior pros I think they understood and respected it. Once I'd said no a few times they left me alone.

The demands of a young boy's obsession with sport set the pattern of family life. Ian and I would be out most nights training and Saturdays were taken up by appearances for Oldham Schools. Because there weren't many kids to call on you could pretty much play all the way through from under-9s, under-11s to under-13s, which meant I was playing both weekend days.

A big kid, I was also quick, and loved kicking a ball. Our coach at the time, Mick Hough, ploughed endless time and energy into skill work. Whenever you saw me from seven years old I had a rugby ball in my hand and was forever passing it. Sometimes Mick would enforce a rule: if we raced ahead in a game and I'd scored a couple of tries I wasn't allowed to score any more. I had to pass. It was clever. It stopped me being one of those big kids who reached fourteen or fifteen and found that everyone had caught them up but didn't have anything else to fall back on. It helped me develop the skills I would need in the professional game. I didn't like it but I understood.

Without hesitation I can say that none of what I've achieved in rugby would have been possible without my parents dedicating themselves to my early years in the endless round of car journeys, practice sessions and matches, often in the weather my part of Lancashire is known for, which I'd summarise as 'wet'.

My dad was an electrician who worked for Norweb, the North Western Electricity Board. He put in a lot of overtime so it was only after the first couple of years that he was there every time, every Sunday on the touchline. My mum was present every single week. In the snow one day, over at Broadbent Road, near to Waterhead, I can remember her walking all the way there and us striding home together in the white haze after the final whistle.

Growing up, I always felt my dad was the disciplinarian, the hard one. The roles now have reversed. My mum's the tougher one. But I never felt she was worried about the risks of us playing such a physical sport. I never detected parental anxiety. She liked the people who would gather at our

15

games and training sessions. She felt at home in that culture.

Both Mum and Dad are quite trade unionist. My dad was a shop steward and my mum was one of the 'Oldham 34' who ended up going to Strasbourg. They stood on a picket line for two years when I was about ten. I can remember how proud my dad was. My mum tells that story in the next chapter. They always wanted us to stand up for what we believed in. And I know how hard it was for them financially. In my own mind, during the strike Mum was still going out to work – but she wasn't. She was standing in the cold at Oldham Hospital and not getting paid.

This was the world that shaped me. Looking back on it sharpens my understanding of an upbringing I might have thought was the norm.

I always felt loved. I always felt that my dad didn't always have the time he wanted to have with us, because he was trying to put food on the table, provide for that annual family holiday, and generally get us to a better position financially. But I never felt as if we – my brother, sister and me – weren't the most important thing to our parents.

The big things in life, or the stuff we craved as kids, came along only occasionally, and we knew not to expect them or take them for granted when they arrived. One Christmas, when I was twelve, Raleigh brought out a new mountain bike, a Raleigh Lizard – light green – and I can remember wanting it and wanting it. Christmas came, and it was mine.

The natural place to keep the bike of your dreams was the shed in the back garden. Two weeks after Christmas, somebody broke in and nicked it. I couldn't get another one.

Where my parents live now is a newer estate. But even as I moved up through the game they wouldn't take anything in the way of financial help. It was always the dream in our part of Saddleworth to end up in Grasscroft. That's where Jayne and I have settled, and I feel very fortunate. I used to get the bus to school and pass through Grasscroft twice a day. I really like the area. Many of my friends live there. Because of its position between Manchester, Huddersfield and Leeds, it's become a desirable commuting spot for people. But it does rain a lot.

Jayne and I were tempted to move out of the area at the end of 2003, when I'd signed a long-term contract at Leeds. The plan at that point was to start looking over in the city where I'd be playing. We'd also decided to have kids. Jayne fell pregnant pretty much straight away so we thought perhaps we'd need the family support to start with, and then go over twelve or eighteen months later. It never happened.

Ten years before, back in 1993, when I signed my first pro contract at thirteen my dad was pretty clued-up and used a financial adviser over in Oldham. Everything I earned was invested. The only part of my new wealth I was allowed to touch was £250 a few years later on my fifteenth birthday. It helped pay for a pair of grey Nike Air Max. Seventy quid. My brother and sister were working at the sports shop where

I bought them. I can remember a guy who owned one of the sports shops in Oldham looking down at my feet and saying, 'What's up with your trainer? Pass it here.' There was nothing wrong with it. He stuck a fork in my air bubble, saying, 'That air bubble's bust.' Got me a brand new pair.

Pride in my appearance was always part of my make-up. Again, much of it came from my brother, who was a bit of a poser in the age of wet-look hair gel.

Back then there were kids in rugby league development teams being paid extravagant amounts. At Lancashire level some of these lads had signed with Wigan or St Helens. They'd all be in fancy kit. One who signed for Wigan was given a cheque for £4,500, which he spent in a week. Among his purchases was a parrot. And the parrot flew straight out through the window.

There were lots of stories like that.

To begin receiving cheques at thirteen allowed me to feel I was making a decent start in life. My dad spent a lot of time fielding calls from agents, mainly. Wigan, Warrington. St Helens came in late, Leeds came in late. Warrington made by far the biggest offer.

Bob Pickles was chief scout at Leeds – Doug Laughton's right-hand man, trying to spot the talent. It was Bob who had to call my dad. To sign with Leeds I went over to the club to meet Doug, but I wouldn't sign the contract there and then. He was taken aback.

'My mum's not here,' I told him.

'Right, if I can get this agreed,' Doug said, 'I'll come to your house tomorrow and you can sign it.'

The next day, I looked through the window and saw his car parked up outside. He had a blue Holden Torana, a cult Australian marque.

You may wonder why I needed my mum to be part of something so straightforward as joining a great rugby club. Even then I was conscious of how much my parents were doing for me and how I needed to involve them in my decisions. I just knew it was important to my mum to be with me when I signed that contract. By that time I was out five nights a week training. Tea wasn't on the table until nine o'clock. I had a sister who was vegetarian. My brother was also training and coming in at different times. From the minute she opened her eyes in the morning, my mum never stopped working or parenting. My dad too. From when I was fourteen he was taking me to Leeds four nights a week, a round trip of a good two hours – a huge strain in a one-car family.

Up Honey Hill strode Doug with the papers. Life was sweet.

It was chance that I ended up at Leeds, where I had no emotional or family connections. We had driven over there to have a look and I could tell Mum and Dad fell in love with the place within minutes of passing through the gates. Back then it was impressive. You had the cricket and rugby grounds, with these big gates at the front. We were bowled over. Getting out of Lancashire was something new and different.

Dougie was the coach, blooding all these new players. At some of the other big clubs I just wasn't sure I'd get the same chance because there were so many kids on the books. Dougie did a really good selling job on us. Ellery Hanley was just about to join Leeds, too. My hero.

When I left school in May 1997 I joined the academy, at under-19 level, and played a few reserve games. The night before my GCSE results dropped, I took a phone call: 'Can you come in for training with the first team tomorrow?'

'Yeah. Course I can.'

Then reality struck: I was meant to be collecting my GCSE results. My parents went off to fetch those and I jumped in a car with Barrie McDermott, who lived locally, and was to become my travelling companion for the next nine years.

So I ended up making my debut at sixteen years old. But that wasn't me permanently planting my flag in the senior starting side. The following week I did my ankle ligaments and was out for three months. At the same time I'd enrolled at Oldham sixth-form college because Mum and Dad were adamant I needed to do my A-levels. The next two years were the toughest of my life, trying to be a full-time rugby league professional and study Maths, Physics, PE and General Studies.

I was growing up fast, and four weeks after my

seventeenth birthday was able to liberate my dad from his endless shuttle runs. Alan McCurrie, the former Oldham hooker, was my driving instructor so I was able to talk rugby all the way through my lessons. It didn't stop me passing the test.

Suddenly I was mobile, driving myself to Leeds four or five nights a week. My dad got some of his life back. And yet I think he secretly missed it. He'd become friendly with one or two of the other dads and would have a natter with them. He'd do a bit of running while I was out there on the pitch. A couple of nights a week he'd get fish and chips from a place in Headingley, which he loved.

Without my mum and dad – no chance. It's so hard for sportspeople who haven't had that sort of time and energy invested in them, especially ones with single parents stretched in all directions. I absolutely couldn't have done it without mine. Dad ended up retiring early and said it was the best thing he ever did, especially for the time it gave him with the grandkids. Four out of the six play rugby, so he's now doing it all again, back in his chauffeur's cap.

People still ask why I didn't just stroll down the road to join Oldham Rugby League Club. And part of the answer is that in those days Oldham weren't looking to sign local boys. I'd been a ballboy there for three years. It might have seemed obvious for me to make that move from retrieving balls to throwing them around in an Oldham shirt. Their fingers, though, had been burned with recent local signings.

It was only when we played Oldham Schools under-16s that Alan McCurrie tried to get me to rip up my Leeds contract. Oldham offered a player swap. Leeds said no. Paul Sculthorpe and Iestyn Harris were among others Oldham missed out on.

Oldham Athletic Football Club did however play a big part in our family life. They were a particularly good side during my childhood years and I remember going to Wembley for the 1990 Littlewoods (or League) Cup final where Nigel Jemson scored the only goal – for Nottingham Forest.

One day I bumped into a guy who had been commercial director at Nottingham Forest, Simon Fotheringham, and he joined us for the Extra Mile. His dad had died of MND and he reached out to us. We got chatting, and I told him, 'You ruined one of the best days of my life.'

'How?' Simon asked.

'You beat us in that Littlewoods Cup final. What's Nigel Jemson doing these days?'

'He's still working at the club.'

'Tell him from me he ruined my childhood.'

A couple of days later Simon sent me a video message from Nigel, returning the playful dig.

* * *

Rugby league wasn't in my blood, but rugby union was never a viable alternative. I was nineteen before I realised there was even a rugby union club in Oldham. It was a decent set-up too. But I have no regrets about following that path into league when I might have ended up in union or even football. Before I joined Leeds, some of the best games of my life were at Waterhead, in the course of a childhood that was full of fun and companionship. There isn't much I'd change. Loved playing with my mates. Loved playing with Oldham Schools on a Saturday, Waterhead on Sunday.

And we were a decent side. There weren't many teams from the Oldham area who would go over to Wigan or St Helens or Warrington and be able to match them. Being in a capable Oldham team that could match the big guns earned you respect.

At Waterhead now, the barbed wire on top of the club-house might suggest a different story, but it's the place where I hit those tackle bags in the mud after drying my tears, and learned about training and fitness, including games of British Bulldog. A lot of running around because it was always freezing. Always with ball in hand we'd play little games of two v. two or three v. three. The pitch sloped massively into a muddy corner where we would aim to kick the ball. We knew how to play that pitch. Then the council levelled it off and our little trick was no use any more.

The club endured tough times. It kept getting broken into, even with the barbed wire. Not that there was much to steal. Players were hard to hold on to. Oldham had nine amateur clubs. Now there are three. Numbers aren't what they should be, but Waterhead have done a tremendous job.

Play well in the morning for Waterhead, then walk the 100 metres to where the Oldham first team then played in the Watersheddings area and be the ballboy. Some of the happiest days of my life. The players had to come down the back of the main stand and into the changing room, right past us. They couldn't escape our adulation. At that time players used to wear tie-ups with their socks, and as soon as the game was finished we, as ballboys, were straight on the field to get the tie-ups of the best players. They were collectors' items. I carried the memory of how precious small items could be into our trilogy of charity runs.

The training, the exposure to the physicality of rugby, caused me no difficulty. I don't remember a bang to the head, or a moment where I felt concussed. Not once did I go home discouraged by the impacts or collisions or aches and pains. Often we'd go and play at the highest school above sea level, on the steep slopes of Saddleworth, where it was always cold, even in sunshine. You had to have an element of toughness about you to play up there.

I've always been confident and believed in my ability as a player, so even at ten I knew I was one of the better kids in my age group. If you watch a lot of kids' sport you'll see that the bigger, dominant September-birthday ones, which I am, tend to get the majority of the ball, and are normally the more powerful children. In rugby, that's going to help. But not necessarily for ever. Not when skills replace size as the most valuable attribute.

I admit I'm concerned that the flow of lads I was part of has slowed in recent years. There are fewer players now than there have ever been. Some of that is down to Covid, some is the attraction of other sports, and part of it reflects the many options people have now to fill their leisure time – it's a cultural change. What hasn't helped is the coverage of the concussion issue. I understand it because I'm a parent myself, and that makes it really difficult to make the right decisions. It makes things tough for contact sports – league and union. At some point though the balance might tip too far, and we'll end up with other societal problems because people aren't exercising or playing team sports.

Nobody can say for certain yet how Rob sadly got what he got. The same with Doddie Weir. The same with Stephen Darby and thousands of others. There are areas where we can reduce or even take away risk, and educate, and ensure players are looked after to a new level. My worry is that in twenty years there's no rugby left, and society has a much bigger problem with, for example, obesity. What rugby gives you I don't think you can get from, say, work.

For league to survive and prosper the kind of communities I grew up in are going to have to keep supplying young players. And not everyone wants to get hit. I haven't seen the player pool numbers since I was at the governing body, the Rugby Football League, but they are quite worrying. The rugby union authorities are also concerned about their numbers.

And yet I think rugby has given me the best things I have in my life. Obviously not my wife and my kids, but everything else. It's not just about the game itself. It's about community. I felt that every step of the way on the trilogy of challenges in support of Rob and others with MND. It's fair to say this strip of the country from Lancashire through Yorkshire has distinctive values that people from other parts of the country might notice when they spend time in this region.

I ought to say that when working at Leicester Tigers in rugby union, I saw the strength of that club and the way the supporters identified with particular values. I've spent time in Newcastle and always think what a brilliant city that is. Cumbria and the Lake District also stand out. Doddie's work in Scotland tells a tale of what people there are like.

But I certainly feel the rugby league belt is a special area. Think how many Olympic gold medals have come out of Yorkshire. Having grown up in Lancashire and played in Yorkshire I do register that strong sense of community. As I began to spend so much more time in Yorkshire, it struck me that people were struggling all the time but happy to find humour in those trials. The people of Leeds will tell you exactly what they think. You either like it or you don't. It's better than the alternative of tip-toeing around things.

If you don't like it, tough, it's off my chest, and you'll have to deal with it.

But when they feel like you're one of their own, they'll come out and stand next to you. They'll fight for you.

People still say good morning up here. Often through gritted teeth, but they still say it.

And when Rob found himself in trouble, those people stepped forward to help.

2

THE SINFIELDS

My mum and dad, Beryl and Ray, are inseparable from my rugby career, my family life now and everything I've done with Rob and MND. I could tell the story of how their political beliefs were part of my upbringing but it's better to let them do it themselves.

So here they are, from the house where my dad has been the archivist of my time in rugby, collecting photos, cuttings and prizes, and where he has many mementoes of his efforts as a proud trade unionist, including a portrait of Che Guevara. That was mentioned once in an article, and every interview after that was all about Cuba and politics. Eventually I was forced to say – I'm not talking about this any more.

First, the rugby . . .

Ray: Kevin was good at sport at school but it never crossed our minds at that stage he would become professional. I know other parents did, and I used to think – where are you coming from? They were young kids.

Beryl: At the time I thought rugby league might be a fad, because he liked football. It was only because Ian came home and said Waterhead were short of players that Kevin said, 'I'd like to go along.' So I thought, well, he can go along and give it a try.

I went a lot. Just to support him. Ray used to work quite hard and Ian would get a lift to his games so with Kevin being the youngest I used to go with him, just really to make sure he was all right.

He was quite poorly when he was born. He had asthma as a baby and the doctor would come in every ten days.

He enjoyed the rugby. He liked going. He made some nice friends.

Ray: To me he always took a leadership role, even as a child. Even at school. If it was a school event, a team, he'd always be there, I think supporting everybody, and encouraging people. I honestly don't know where he got it from.

From when Kevin was about twelve we started to get tapped up at games. They were a good team, Waterhead, probably one of the top two in Lancashire, on this side of the Pennines. We felt it was much too early to think about it as a professional career or commit to one club.

We put them off as much as we could, saying we'd look at it again in twelve months or two years. It got to the stage where we got tired of it. The phone was ringing every weekend.

Warrington basically said to us: what do you want for us to sign Kevin? I know it sounds ridiculous. There would have been an upper limit. At the time we were very naive and had no idea what to ask for. In later years you gain more knowledge. When we decided we needed to cut out the phone calls and cut out the pressure on Kevin we took some advice from ex-pros and other people.

When we went to Leeds I certainly felt that was the right place for him.

When Leeds were contacting us and others were pestering us we said we don't want Kevin to sign for anyone yet, and they said, 'OK, we'll leave you be. We won't pester you, but don't sign for anyone else without speaking to us.' Which we respected.

At the time it was a feeling more than anything else. We went to Leeds, spoke to the scouts, spoke to Dougie Laughton. It just felt right.

When he got into the academy it was a great team with great parents. It was such a good atmosphere. And Leeds put on social events for the parents, like going bowling. There was a bit of camaraderie. Kevin used to do his training and I'd do a few laps round the cricket field.

The Oldham 34, and life on the picket line . . .

Beryl: After leaving my job at Birch Hall hotel, I worked nights from ten till three, looking after doctors and nurses with meals. The old Oldham Royal closed and they said we could be deployed to the new hospital. I got a job in psychiatric outpatients, on reception. Computerisation came in, and they promised a pay rise, but only the shop stewards got one, so we all voted to come out on strike, because I thought it was the right thing to do.

I was on strike for almost two years from 1990 to 1991. We went all over the country speaking. I went to Strasbourg to speak to the European Parliament. We became known as the Oldham 34. Quite a lot of the workers went back, but the ones who had been there a long time stayed out. There were 110 of us medical staff, but it dropped down to sixty-eight, then thirty-four, as people found other jobs. While I was at the picket line, Stephanie brought her O-level results to me.

We didn't win. I got a letter through the post, hand-delivered. It said: if you're not at work by nine o'clock tomorrow you'll be sacked. They sacked us the next day and drafted in agency staff immediately. It was like a family there. The consultants used to come up and say, 'Just come back, we'll make sure you're looked after.' But we stuck with the main body. I stayed out till the end.

It was awful. Then the union said, 'We're not going to go

anywhere with this now, if you want to retrain . . .' That's when I went to a commercial college in Oldham and learned shorthand and computers.

Activism . . .

Ray: Kevin got dragged all over the place. He got dragged to miners' strike collection points, CND [Campaign for Nuclear Disarmament] demonstrations in London, anti-apartheid demonstrations in London. We lost him in Hyde Park a couple of times. He used to wander off.

Beryl: Stephanie and I used to go to Greenham Common [the site of the Women's Peace Camp] every Christmas with a group from Oldham and take food parcels down.

Ray: The electricians' union got kicked out of the TUC [Trades Union Congress] over the Wapping dispute and we formed another union. I was heavily involved in that for many years. Local campaigns, CND, anti-apartheid. I helped to run the local miners' campaign. I have pictures of Kevin with collection buckets. He used to join us. He had no choice. He had to be somewhere.

I like to think the politics rubbed off on Kevin. I always thought my children would follow my views and politics. I thought it was just a given. I don't know why but I just did. We always discussed politics in the home.

My brother Ian and sister Steph . . .

Ray: Our big thing with Kevin and his brother and sister was – you've got to be honest. Not just honest as a person but honest when you're dealing with other people.

Ian's had it tough at times. He's often said he's had a lot of rubbish thrown in his face, like, 'You're shit, you're not as good as your brother, you're living on your brother's coat-tails,' but he's always been really supportive of Kevin.

Stephanie is a geography teacher, at Bluecoat in Oldham. She went for rugby trials with Hull women but somebody broke a hip in the first session and she said, 'That's not for me.'

Having a well-known son . . .

Beryl: We were very, very proud, but we just kept our feet on the ground.

Ray: I'm proud of all my three children. I am. I'm proud of what they've done. I'm proud of the people they are. Kevin no more than the other two. But Kevin's done certain things where you think . . . wow.

Beryl: You get a bit embarrassed sometimes, don't you.

Ray: I do. I find I meet my own work-mates now and all they want to talk about is Kevin. And I feel like saying,

'Yeah, but how about me [laughing]? I'm Ray Sinfield, I've got a life as well you know [still laughing].' But I don't mean that in a negative way, because it's really nice when people do want to talk about Kevin, and we are proud. It's a strange one. There've been so many moments when we've seen him lifting trophies and we've seen him on TV. You're just bursting with pride.

Working with Rob . . .

Beryl: It sounds a bit gushy, but Kevin would help anybody if he could, as would we. Yeah, we'd help people, but it's certainly gone way beyond our imagination. It's phenomenal.

Ray: When I look back on it now, what Kevin has done since he finished rugby means far more to me than what he did when he played rugby. All the honours, all the trophies were great at the time. But to see what he's tried to do in his charity work . . . I just feel it's worth so much more, to me. I'm just so proud of him. I'm more proud of him because of that. The type of person he is, that's what makes me more proud. This is something above rugby, something more than that.

Rob's dad Geoff and I have known each other for a long, long while. Geoff was involved in the trade union movement as well so we got on quite well. Nice people. They're a nice family. How could you not like Rob as well, for what he was. The size of him. You had to admire him as a player. And what he's doing now is mind-blowing. To be that sort of person, and how he's fought what he's going through . . .

I've tried to speak to Rob's dad about it but it's really hard. We had a couple of phone conversations that didn't go well. He was upset, then the second time I got upset. It's very hard to get your feelings across.

The Seven in Seven and the Extra Mile . . .

Ray: We found it quite overwhelming.

Beryl: It was hard seeing him struggling back from that 101 miles. That last bit when he came into Headingley . . .

Ray: I was a bit worried when his quads went in the 101 miles. I thought – Christ, how's he going to get through this? We tried to stay positive with Jayne. I have to say I never thought for one minute he wouldn't complete either challenge. I thought, he'll crawl if he has to.

Beryl: The butcher said to me, 'What's he going to do next?'
    I said, 'I don't know.'
    And he said, 'It'll have to be bigger than the 101.'
    And I couldn't imagine what that would be. If someone tells Kevin he can't do something, he'll do it.

Ray: The thing that strikes me about Kevin is, what you see with him is what you get. It doesn't matter whether he's on TV, coaching kids or sat here with us. To me, he never changes, his persona never changes, he never ever strikes me as putting on any kind of act. It's just him.

The Ultra 7 in 7 . . .

Ray: When we heard Kevin was moving on to seven ultra-marathons we took it in our stride – because we know that's what he's like. I didn't question it until nearer the time, when I thought – gee, that's a bit optimistic. But Kevin's Kevin and he'll do what he wants.

We were a bit worried, a bit concerned, as all parents would be.

The medical side was well covered, which reassured us, and the people who did it with him were such good friends that I knew they would look after each other. It was refreshing for us to know he wouldn't be on his own and would have that support, which is essential to complete something like that.

He's happiest in a team environment. That was always the case when he was young. After the ultra-marathons Kevin had a letter from a guy who used to train him at Lancashire with the under-13s. He said he'd been asked who was the best kid who'd been through his ranks and he always said Kevin. Then he was asked why, and he would reply – looking after other people, being part of the team.

So it's always been part of Kevin's mantra, what moves him, what motivates him.

On the ultras we went up to see him at the Rams Head pub on the moors above Saddleworth, where he and the team took a break. I never doubted he'd see it through. I thought he'd have to fall or pull something for him not to complete the challenge.

I found the reception he got at Old Trafford at the end very emotional. Incredible. I hadn't experienced anything as emotional as that at a sports event. A lot of people have said, 'You must have been really proud.' Yeah. It was more than proud. It was a very emotional experience for us.

I'm in awe of him because of what he's done, but in another way he's just Kevin. I'm used to him acting like that. He's a very caring human being. That's what motivates him and it's what makes us very happy and proud.

People ask me, 'What's he doing next?'

I say, 'I don't know, but he'll think of something.'

3

LEADERSHIP

Rugby hooked me quickly, but ten was the age when I knew there was more to it than just enjoying the game. I found the door to captaincy, to leadership, and my whole career would be shaped from then on by my urge to influence more than just my own performance.

It was a day, a single game, that awakened those instincts. Every season there'd be county selections for Lancashire to play Yorkshire and Humberside. The first year I made the grade was under-9s. But not in the starting team. They'd put me on the bench for a game in Hull.

I remember dwelling on that during the long bus journey over.

The game unfolds and I get five minutes on the pitch at the end.

I say to myself, 'I'll never come up here and be on the bench again.'

The following year I was made captain.

It sounds crazy to be disappointed at nine years old with five minutes' playing time, but I really did come home thinking: this is not happening to me again, I'm not having this.

The following year I returned for Lancashire trials. It's as vivid to me as yesterday. We were separated into teams. I was in an Orrell St James kit, looking round the team I'd been allocated to, thinking: we're going to get hammered here; I've got to find a way to make sure I'm in the Lancashire team next time and not on the bench.

We played three twenty-minute blocks and I spent the whole hour playing as well as I could but also encouraging everyone around me. I was dependent on everyone playing well for me to get where I wanted to go: the Lancashire starting side.

That was the day I realised how powerful it was to talk to people during games; how communicating could elevate performance. It wasn't just me who benefited. The vast majority of that team were subsequently picked for Lancashire – against the odds. I was made captain of the county side. And that was the point at which I made the vital correlation: helping to get the most out of those around me would also help me play better and get the most out of me. It was all connected.

So now I'm in the Lancashire team as captain, knowing I can do something with this.

It was young to be arriving at such a profound realisation.

Regularly I'm asked about being a captain and the secrets of leadership. It's a fascination for many people who love sport. I led the team at Leeds Rhinos for thirteen years and also captained England. People ask, 'What's that about, where does it come from?'

I don't struggle for an answer: 'It happened one day back in Orrell, when I was ten. That's how I did it.'

An individual having a galvanising effect on a team is spotted straight away by coaches and team-mates. Once you've demonstrated the ability to make a difference the label is pinned to you. I was happy to wear it. Pretty much every time I played from the age of ten I ran out as captain.

So what was I doing, what was I telling our team to give them impetus? In those early years it was pure encouragement. Much of that derived from my upbringing, from my mum and dad. Also from my Waterhead coach Mick Hough, who was semi-pro (he was a long-distance lorry driver) and had some really good values about him. The heart of his coaching method was to encourage us all the time.

It might have gone either way. Had we been a flop and a failure in that trial at Orrell the chance might have been taken away from me. Any leadership qualities I had might have been deprived of the opportunity to shine. The armband would have been thrown to another lad. I might have been denied further chances to test myself in that wider realm of trying to have a positive effect on others (not that

I was the only one who took on those responsibilities at Leeds).

At Rhinos, with my reputation from youth rugby, I always felt they'd marked me out as a potential captain of the senior team. At sixteen I led the under-19s. I really shouldn't have captained a side three years up the age scale. I think they did it to ruffle feathers in the group and to challenge me to see whether I was capable of it. When I made my first-team debut at sixteen I know Leeds would have faced resentment from some other parents. 'My son's been here two or three years, why isn't he getting the chance?'

My attitude was: I'll show you. No matter how good a player you are, there's always someone who wants to have a crack at you. I stopped trying to please everyone a long time ago. As long as the people who matter are happy, I'm all right with that.

I was twenty-two when I was made first-team captain. Iestyn Harris had been a fine leader but had moved to Wales. Franny Cummins took over and was brilliant with me. He spent a lot of time helping me through as a first-team player. As did Barrie McDermott. After Iestyn, they tried a couple of captains. Then Daryl Powell became head coach. I'd played with him. He was my first roomie – a 35-year-old with a seventeen-year-old. Daryl made the step up to coach and put the call in to me. I think the club knew we had assembled a strong young core group, with no baggage, who hadn't had Wigan's constant success rammed down their throats for years and years. It was a fresh start. By then I was an international player and the club felt confident giving the armband to an up-and-coming youngster.

But first, I needed to make my own call – to Franny. 'I don't want to accept this if you're not on board,' I told him. His reply couldn't have been more encouraging: 'Kev, you're the right man for the job, I'll be right behind you.' When the captain you're replacing backs you unconditionally you know you have a chance. I knew I'd make some mistakes and get stuff wrong, but I never felt the senior Leeds players weren't behind me.

I was seen as mature for my age, perhaps because I'd spent so much time growing up with my older brother and his mates. One of my methods has always been to put myself in the shoes of others and understand how they feel. It's helped me in coaching too. I never forget what it's like to put your boots on and be out there playing, and how all the elements of being a professional player test you.

In the week leading up to rugby union's Premiership final between Leicester and Saracens in June 2022, I knew there were players who'd be disappointed at being left out for a game that would crown the champions of England. It helps when you've been to that lonely place where you're told you won't be taking part. I've missed finals and been dropped. That never leaves you.

I was left out for my first Challenge Cup final when I was nineteen. I'd played every game that year, won man of the match in the semi-final in Huddersfield, and scored a couple of tries the week before the final. On the Wednesday leading in, coach Dean Lance pulled me aside. 'I'm going with someone else,' he said. 'You're not experienced enough.'

It was a cop-out. Which nineteen-year-old in the country is experienced enough?

Over time you come to understand that it's easier to upset a nineteen-year-old than an older player. My world fell apart. But it was one of the best things that could have happened to me. It took a while, but finally I was able to see that it wasn't the disaster I'd built it up to be. I'd thought that my world was ending. To me it meant going home to tell Mum and Dad I wasn't good enough. When they say you're not experienced enough, that's an easy way of letting you down.

My tortured mind was straightened out from an unlikely source.

The teams have jogged out, the game is about to start, and I'm emotional, with full eyes. The pre-match entertainer for the final is Tony Hadley of Spandau Ballet. Tony finishes his set and is looking for a place to sit. He ends up parking himself near me and a chat begins. Tony's casting his gaze on a nineteen-year-old who's obviously upset. He asks me what's troubling me and I tell him the story.

'I've been left out, I've played every game this year, and blah blah blah.'

Tony says to me, 'If you think that's bad . . .'

He had a few bits of his own going on. His wife had left him. The band had split up. He had financial problems. It snapped me out of the state I was in. Suddenly, by comparison, life didn't seem so bad.

But to miss out on a final is murder. You get your new suit, everyone's family and friends are going to the game, you meet up with the team, it's cup final day at a big stadium . . . but you're not playing. You're a spectator.

When that 2000 final was over, an early night felt like a good option. I'd had enough. And I didn't get back in the team for nearly a month.

It would be overstating it to say I'd had it all my own way up to that point, but I certainly wasn't an expert on dealing with setbacks. I wasn't equipped to cope with or understand this one.

It happened a couple of times in my career. Each time it was horrible. My personality just wasn't suited to that level of rejection, or disappointment. Yet each time there were lessons to set against the misery.

People get left out for all sorts of reasons. In the week of that Leicester–Saracens final in 2022 I had a conversation with one of our young players who hadn't been selected. I talked to him about how tough the weekend was going to be and tried to help him find a way to enjoy it. My message was: next time you're here you'll be focused as a member of the starting team and won't be able to take in the crowd, so absorb everything you can now, and learn from it. And if we're lucky enough to get a winner's medal, don't devalue it.

I certainly did that in my own playing career. If I hadn't played, I took a dim view of my winner's medal, though I kept them all. My parents, who had a broader perspective on it, hoarded everything. I lost five Challenge Cup finals as captain. So, by the time I'd been beaten in five I was starting to think: bloody hell, I'd best cherish the winner's medal I earned, even if it was from a game I wasn't selected for.

The 1999 Challenge Cup, which Leeds won, was the first year I missed out. But that year I'd been on the fringe and hadn't expected to play. In 2000, when we lost 24–18 to Bradford Bulls, I was dropped, pure and simple. It wasn't easy, but over time I learnt to understand the value of the squad, and how a united dressing room helps you prepare better and keep the squad environment healthy. So you're supportive of the guys who take to the field – even if you don't.

Comprehending that lesson has been a big part of my journey in sport, and I try to pass it on. I wouldn't be able to preach the fact that squad players are vitally important had I not experienced being on the margins in my own career. You have to have lived it to talk about it with any credibility to a young player who's heartbroken at not making the starting team.

At Leicester I found myself having what you might call deep and meaningful conversations with players. I didn't force my own history on them. They came to me. It was lovely. Some of them watched rugby league, but many of the younger lads wouldn't have seen much of my career. As they started to ask questions, I was able to say, 'Yeah, I was left out of a final too.' I was able to offer them a bit of context.

The best assistant coaches can be a link to the head coach, not by being 'soft ears' but in reinforcing the head coach's message while helping players to refocus, perhaps after a disappointment. Firm but fair is the combination you're aiming for. And you'll find yourself explaining how selection actually works, how permutations might have worked against them, and why being left out isn't a personal rejection.

Before the 2022 Premiership final, Steve Borthwick had to get round forty blokes to explain the chosen team in a very short space of time. Often the only words they hear are 'you're in' or 'you're not in'. They don't want to hear the rest. A lot of the work from then on is putting people back together. Helping them understand. Making everyone aligned again.

*   *   *

As Mum and Dad explained in Chapter 2, I grew up in a household that was very socialist. The feeling of us all being in it together will have shaped my sense of what captaincy or leadership is about. Maybe not consciously, but those values we had at home would have soaked in.

We had race riots in Oldham in 2001. It ripped the town open. But in our household it was drilled into us as kids that the colour of someone's skin didn't matter. I was fully aware of that all through my childhood. I attended Oldham sixth-form college, which was culturally diverse. You can't grow up in Oldham and not have an understanding of and respect for other cultures. You were aware that some households retained archaic views about race, but I was able to start out without any of those prejudices.

In the first Leeds team we had two black players who, alongside Barrie McDermott, were our enforcers: Anthony Farrell and Darren Fleary. Leeds had always had black players. I can't imagine being in a dressing room where it's acceptable to discriminate against anyone or treat them differently.

I always felt my role as captain was to get the best out of people and I understood from an early age that people had different backgrounds, characters and personalities. The dressing room needed a bit of everything – including the eccentricity or even wildness of some of the men I played with. Sometimes you need the unexpected. Between us, we fostered an environment where we wanted to help one another and trusted one another. We didn't talk about it in theoretical terms. But we all knew it was there. That's what our team was built on.

There's a saying associated with me, even though I'm not certain I actually said it: 'You end up an average of the five people you spend most time with.' Jamie Jones says it all the time about me – though I actually think it came from him. What do I mean by it? Let's turn it round. It's more that if you spend too much time with the wrong people you'll take wrong turns.

The great advantage I had at Leeds was to have a collection of strong lieutenants. Jamie Peacock was already a full international captain. The young lads had all come through together – Danny McGuire, Jamie Jones – and knew how to strive as one. International regulars peppered the side, for example Danny Buderus (Australia) and the Samoan Willie Poching. Barrie McDermott captained Ireland.

A fine mix of leaders. At any one time I was more than happy for one of them to lead, provided the team came first. And in plenty of circumstances they were better than me. The value of shared leadership became more and more apparent. I had the 'c' next to my name and led the side out, lifted the trophies, but I never felt this is 'my' team and I'm in control of it. It was *our* team. We looked after it together.

In the search for a winning mentality I'd use the see-saw analogy. In any dressing room you need a critical mass of people who want to win and will make the necessary sacrifices. Without that core, you'll go up and down on the see-saw, having good days and bad.

In any team there's always a group in the middle who will follow the crowd. In each dressing room there are character flaws that work against what the team are trying to do. But you can carry those imperfections if the heart of the side is a group who know where they're going and won't take no for an answer.

We'd try to do it the right way and treat people properly. Sometimes that meant not getting it right and losing games, but there was always some integrity about the way those Leeds teams went about their business.

I'm not the confrontational type. But in games and training, standards were important to me, and I was happy to call people out. I'd do the same to myself. In front of people. You have to be able to display honesty to demand it from other people. We also had strong head coaches who were more than willing to point the finger. If a coach had gone hard on somebody it was often my job to pull them back together and get them back on board, to explain what the coach had meant.

Most people don't go looking for confrontation. But for a team to progress, it has to be part of the mix. In rugby league, there's no hiding. If you're standing in the shadows, hoping not to be too involved, it's obvious to everyone around you.

And you'll get hurt, if you're not ready for contact, or you shy away from it. If you go into a challenge and you're not committed to it, you can come off badly. We always used the term 'body in front'. Get your torso out front so you have the initiative in the tackle. At Leicester Tigers that principle was harder to apply. In rugby union now the laws are about lowering the height of tackles.

You may wonder whether I ever just wanted a quiet day at work, a game that didn't hurt, a routine win with no drama or pain the next day. The answer is: often. I played just short of 600 games. Matches are preceded by days of preparation that go unseen. Just over a year and a half of my life was spent getting ready for rugby games. So absolutely there were times when I thought, 'I don't fancy it today.' Especially when I woke up with a niggle or something not feeling right. Or if I felt a bit 'off'.

The challenge for me was to turn that round, to dissolve those thoughts by the time the whistle blew.

I wasn't a stranger to self-doubt. I've sat in dressing rooms, for Grand Finals, looked around at the internationals sat with me and thought, 'What am I doing in here? That guy over there can do this, him over there can do that.' Your mind plays tricks on you.

Self-doubt is hard to rationalise or justify. The amount of energy wasted on introspection is high. When I think of the endless prep time, how hard I worked, how meticulous I was, it wasn't logical to question my right to belong in those changing rooms. But sometimes I did.

Perhaps in the later years it was my way of keeping myself on my toes, making sure I was ready to play. These were uncertainties that crept in twenty minutes before we ran out. It's easy to be distracted by negative thoughts in a hotel the night before, but when you're staring down the barrel of running out in front of 70,000 people, twenty minutes before kick-off, it's not helpful.

The bigger the occasion, the bigger the scope for uneasiness. With all respect to the lesser nations at international level, it would manifest itself most sharply against Australia or New Zealand. Domestically, against St Helens, Wigan or Bradford, in those early years, when there were big crowds, large TV audiences.

A captain's job can be lonely. We didn't often stay in hotels because we played along that M62 corridor, but for Grand Finals I had a friend at the Midland Hotel in Manchester who would look after me with a room to myself. It was lovely. But over time I realised I didn't want that. I'd have been better with a team-mate in a single bed next to me who I could bounce things off and chat to about non-rugby things.

The last game of my Rhinos career, the 2015 Grand Final at Old Trafford, stands out as a memory of my thoughts trying to sabotage me. I can still visualise being in the dressing room and thinking: this could go really badly today. The game was built up as us clinching the Treble. My final game. The perfect goodbye. And yet part of my mind was saying: this could end up horrendous today. I don't suppose that's uncommon. Admitting to it, though, goes against the grain of how we see people at the top level in sport.

That's something else I've tried to pass on in my coaching career, just before games. In a dressing room you can see the strain on people's faces. You try to take that away by normalising it. Sometimes as a coach I'd say, 'You may not remember me playing because I'm a long time retired, but actually I went through and felt exactly what you're going through and feeling now. It's normal. What you've got to do is get rid of it as quickly as you can.'

I always took comfort in those around me. I needed eye contact; I needed to get up and speak to my team-mates, look them in the eye. Often I could see in them the fear I was experiencing. That helped. Regardless of the armband and the authority the job bestows, a captain is just like everyone else.

4

MY FRIEND ROB

There was this little kid from Castleford. So quick, but tiny. Too small, most people thought, to make a Leeds Rhinos player. He didn't say a lot either – at first. But he made up for that later.

Small rugby league players weren't unheard of. Half-backs tended to be on a more modest physical scale. But Rob was minuscule. You would look at the average twelve-year-old prospect and think: 'He'll grow.' But then you looked at Rob Burrow's mum and dad and thought: 'He probably *won't* grow.'

There were only two in Rob's age group. The other was Danny McGuire. In my age category, two years up, there were four. But against all the odds, Rob stood out. My memories of him then are all based on how fast he was. At first there was no personal connection, no solidarity built around how young we were. We were all shy kids, in awe of the people who were running around, so there was no attempt to strike up conversation.

53

In the mid-1990s, Leeds were good at getting every age group together once a month for a club training night. You had first team, reserves, academy and any other kid who'd signed professional forms. There'd be a four-skill rotation. You might be in a group with Garry Schofield or Ellery Hanley – giants of the game. Or you could have found yourself working with a Rob Burrow, who was twelve years old at the time.

As in those childhood days at Waterhead, when I was an Oldham ballboy marvelling at the first-team players, I was starstruck by the big names around me. Signing professional forms didn't make me any less in awe. Some unbelievable players were moving around in my vision, sharing the grass I was on, playing for the same club as me.

For somebody as small as Rob to succeed in that environment they needed a super skill – and he had one. His pace. Not top-end speed but an ability to change direction, and a sidestep. Nobody could get near him. It was this elusive little kid zipping around a field of big men – men who could deal with most things, but not darting speed.

If you were looking for a player to compare Rob to in his teenage years it would be Jason Robinson, a star for Wigan throughout the 1990s who went on to win a rugby union World Cup with England in 2003. Jason had a wonderful career and might have beaten Rob on top-end pace, but I reckon Rob would have come out top on agility drills.

For the first couple of years of our time as fellow hopefuls

I would see Rob only once a month. He was still fourteen when I joined the academy at sixteen. He'd take part in the odd session but socially he was too young to take much notice of. At that stage I'd have been closer to Barrie McDermott and the lads in my slightly older age group.

The academy side would always play before the first team on a Friday night and often the first team would turn up early to watch the young lads. We won umpteen academy finals, yet not many players were making it through to first-team level. We needed to change that. I hadn't played academy all year, but I was still eligible when the academy lads reached a final at St Helens.

Desperate to win, they brought me back to play in it.

I was embarrassed. I hadn't played for them in the whole campaign, and now someone was going to lose their place to me. A couple of others also dropped back down from the first-team squad to increase our chances of winning.

Rob played in that game. And that was the first time I played a full match with him. Straight away I could see it. 'This lad can play.' I'd watched him do his thing from the touchline, but to actually share space with him in a game was a revelation.

When he appeared on the edge of the first team around 2001, it was our chance to form a lasting friendship. In 2001–02 we moved training grounds, and sitting next to me in the changing room, by chance, was . . . Rob Burrow. Typically he would turn up for training in a pair of boxer shorts.

He never brought a towel. Never brought a bag. And back then you washed your own kit. As soon as training was finished he was gone. Wanted to get home. He was a big film buff. *Championship Manager* was big at the time and that also absorbed his attention when he was away from the club. He was a fan of American football too. Very often you would still be on the training pitch and Rob would be driving out of the car park. In many ways he was a model pro, but in others you would struggle to make that claim for him because he didn't do 'extras'.

Then again, he didn't need to. There weren't aspects of his game where you thought: he needs to work on this and work on that. The bits he should have done extras for were the bits he didn't have in the first place, if that makes sense. So in his own mind he had it all worked out, and he would shoot off straight after training, knowing that players who do that open themselves up to grumbling and resentment. But he had an answer for anyone who might question the way he operated. When it came to the drills and testing, he won everything.

In the conventional sense you wouldn't have thought of him as central to 'the group'. More as an eccentric or individualist who was good to have on your side. Prominent among my memories of him is a session we did at Roundhay Park, up a brutal hill that Leeds still use to push fitness up a notch or two. We had some horrendous sessions on that hill.

Rob had bought a bright red MR2. He was about

twenty-three. Nobody else at the club had a flashy sports car. We drove out of Roundhay car park after one of these savage sessions and Rob's fancy car is on its side. I have Barrie McDermott in my car with me. 'Shit, that's Rob's car.' He even had a private reg, so it wasn't hard to identify. As we approach, Rob slithers out of the window. He doesn't open the door. That would have been too conventional. It was one of those movie scenes where everyone thinks the car is about to blow. The big oak tree he'd crashed into had a huge dent in it. Rob, on the other hand, was undamaged.

Once the shyness recedes, young lads start to stick together. I'd made it my business to try to help Rob settle into life as a future first-team player. There was another youngster in Rob's age group who, by contrast, was a giant of a man – Chev Walker. Chev also tried to guide Rob. There was an exceptional togetherness among the young players that was to become the foundation of a lot of success for the club.

You didn't see Rob's true nature straight away. When he spoke he did so with a nervousness, really fast. His words tumbled out. As time went on we started to see his personality, his humour.

Away from the dressing room he was a private guy. When we'd won a Grand Final we would always get together for a day afterwards. I was never a big drinker but I'd always go. Sometimes I would drive, have the day with the lads, then come away. Rob would have two beers – then, gone.

You would ring him on his mobile. No answer.

He would always go home.

Home was his sanctuary.

There was a part of him, I believe, that felt drink was a poison that would stop him being as good as he wanted to be. Then again this was a bloke who was addicted to Red Bull and Coke. He loved caffeine, all the time. He'd have double espressos, six or seven a day, which made him talk quicker – even faster than he talked already.

Rob said in his own book that signing for Leeds meant joining 'the big city slickers'. That made me giggle. As a Lancashire lad who had crossed the county line I had a more objective view of Yorkshire politics. I could understand it from him, growing up in 'Cas', because they hate Leeds there. Cas people think Leeds are arrogant – a charge directed at most trophy-winning clubs. When Rob and I signed in that two- to three-year period in the mid-1990s, Leeds hadn't won anything for a long time, and were sleeping giants – but they had spent a lot of money to turn that image round.

Athletically, pound for pound, Rob was as strong as anyone in the gym, like a little gymnast. On the field he was superb at getting away from people who were hunting him down. His agility and speed would carry him away from the monsters. Added to that were his natural skills and a good left foot. He was a goal kicker, and very creative. He wasn't a schemer who'd be trying to pull people out of position and put team-mates through gaps. It was more that natural gas carried him to places where he bought time for himself to use his skill set to then pick passes.

The schemer type is the slower sort of player. That was me. I was nowhere near as quick as Rob. I had to find another way of manipulating defences. Rob would just scare them to death.

The rapport between us deepened in 2003, when Rob was picked a lot by Daryl Powell for first-team games. By 2004 he was pretty much our first-choice scrum-half. The balance flipped from two or three lads in the senior side to a massive senior group of ten lads who were under twenty-three. For some of the older hardcore it must have been unsettling to face such an influx of youth. Some found their place in the team under threat. But they embraced it, got on with it, and helped those younger players flourish. They seemed to love having us around.

Rob could always be trusted on the pitch. He was tough. Extremely tough. A guy of his proportions had to be. He would make you laugh because relative to size he was the fittest and strongest in every test. But every morning at training he would fret about the sessions planned for that day. Each time he would ask the strength and conditioning coach what the session was going to look like, because he'd be anxious about what was coming his way.

I'd look at him thinking: what are you worried about? You're going to win anyway. There's not a scrap on you. You're muscle on muscle. What are you bothered about?

Like me, Rob was a pleaser who didn't want to be in trouble.

Don't get me wrong, he worked hard, but some of those bits I and some of the other players had to do, Rob didn't have to do.

I don't begrudge him that at all.

He made the best of what he had. The coaches understood his super strength, which was his ability to turn a game on its head through a flash of brilliance, together with his deft left foot. He was a game-changer. There were lots of times when he made the difference between us winning or losing, whether starting or off the bench. You always felt there was a moment from him, if you needed it. Of all the different make-ups of players, he was one of our best defenders as well because he would use his pace to save himself and relieve the pressure on the rest of us.

Because of the momentum of some of the opponents running at him – and the weight difference – Rob had to get underneath the ball carrier to give himself a chance, and he'd shock people with the effectiveness of his tackling, which was based on that technique of getting right below the runner's centre of gravity.

And yes, I did worry about the physical impact on him of his tackling. Like many players of that era he went through a spell of wearing a headguard. But it only seemed to make him more of a target. I don't know why, but with his scrumcap on there seemed to be more collisions involving his head.

Although it was Rob's idea to wear the headguard, part of him hated having it on. Big shoulder pads also became part of his armour. There was a fashion for headguards and shoulder pads in the mid-1990s – I gave them a try – and they stuck around for a generation because kids bought them and were determined to get their money's worth. I don't think they made much difference. There was a period too when everyone wore shin pads.

The big men were scared of Rob's ability to leave them for dead. So they wanted him off the pitch. They went after him – when they could get their hands on him. They went after the little scamp to stop him embarrassing them and to suppress the talent he had for turning defence into attack.

By the time Rob was diagnosed with motor neurone disease, we'd been through all the stages of playing together. Each one brought us closer. You don't articulate it or tell each other you're climbing the friendship scale. Words don't define it. Shared experience forms the bond.

An example: I hold the record for most Challenge Cup final losses as a captain. Five. Rob was in all five of those teams. It's just me and him in that category. It became a curse that nagged away at us both. Although we'd lost the full five, there were others who'd lost three and four, so we were in respectable company. On big media days journalists mined the line – 'Your careers won't be complete if you don't win a Challenge Cup, will they.' I spent my whole time batting it back: no, my career's complete, if it happens, it happens, blah blah blah.

But I was desperate to win it. Desperate.

On all five occasions we were beaten by the better side. Each time we were also fighting hard in the league while trying to win the Challenge Cup. Much later, the Australian coach Wayne Bennett gave me a great image. He said: 'It's really difficult to fight on two fronts. You have to decide which one you're going for. Otherwise you could end up in the middle of the doughnut, with nothing.'

It takes people a while to work out that doughnut analogy. But you can see what he meant.

You spend a lot of time sat in dressing rooms with the people you go into action with, a lot of time in pre-season, in tough sessions, where the chat flows.

'We need to get this right.'

'Oh Christ, we've got this horrible session ahead of us.'

It all builds up.

Throughout those gruelling days you're always building. Relationships are forged by the intensity of the time you're spending together – time when you're always pushing your body further than it wants to go. Four years together is like forty. You're going to places most people don't go. And you're seeing your mate suffering the same way you are. This was my life at Leeds with Rob – and with many others.

When Rob finished playing and we were working together on the staff at Leeds we were still like team-mates. When I first went back to Leeds, in 2018 as director of rugby, Rob came in and wanted to coach our half-backs and spend some time with them, which gave me time to do other work. But I wanted our pathway coaches to spend time with the first team. I wanted the club to be joined up and aligned so it was easier for players to come through the stages. Early on I cut him a fair bit of slack because I knew he was transitioning from player to coach. You go from being at the club six hours a day to being there for twelve. Or that's the expectation.

That year, Rob and I were given a chance to spend precious time together, the sort you don't often get. Leeds had been in a relegation scrap. We'd organised a ten-day break after a vital game in London to look at potential pre-season camps for the following campaign. Rob, the head of performance Jason Davidson and I flew to France for two nights. A brilliant trip. We took a look at two training facilities that we were thinking of booking. It was a great road tour: a stag trip without the beer. We just laughed for two days.

It was a new kind of time I was spending with Rob. It wasn't dressing room or club time. We were just mates on an adventure. We weren't to know we were building an extra layer of friendship that we'd later draw on when Rob's life became unrecognisable.

5

THE ETERNAL TEAM:
MY RUGBY LEAGUE CAREER

Anyone who has had a career in professional sport looks back with amazement. Life after playing is often unrecognisable from the tunnel vision of being out there on the pitch. Sometimes you can hardly believe that was you, that was what you did. But all the while the experiences are shaping you for what comes after, good or bad.

So much has happened to me since I stopped playing rugby that it can be hard to transport myself back to the intensity of games that came thick and fast, and tests that were a daily feature of life – and which you had to rise to.

But in my story there's a strong connection between the first and second halves of my life. The bridge is team, friendship, solidarity. Forming bonds at Leeds Rhinos was laying the groundwork for lifelong ties after the rugby stopped. Those attachments had a second role in the work we've done to fight MND.

But first I had to work out what really mattered to me in rugby, how I was going to operate, what strengths I could bring. And I could only do that in the context of those around me, those I'd fought the battles with. My success was inseparable from theirs. In this account of my playing days I hope you'll see the connections and understand how my career flowed into the new challenges I've taken on.

The story of Leeds Rhinos in a golden era for the club wasn't just about Rob and me. My core of friends were his mates too. They all deserve recognition in any account of how an extraordinary group of people won so many trophies.

The first player I looked up to and wanted to emulate was Ellery Hanley, who became a friend after he presented me with a Super League player of the month award in 2005. That was my first real contact with a man I'd seen as the ultimate rugby star.

I loved the way he moved, the way he played the game, the way he carried himself, the respect everyone seemed to have for him. He was the player everyone wanted to play alongside. When I speak to referees, they mention how Ellery spoke to them, how he tried to get them onside. I tried to grab on to that. I was the polite type of captain: yes sir, no sir. Ellery had ways of asking loaded or rhetorical questions and was very smart.

I had a lighthouse eye for the qualities I wanted in my own game, and the strengths others could bring. The gifts

Rob had were among the ingredients in that winning recipe. If I were calling some of the great team-mates I had up on to a stage, this is how I might announce them . . .

*　*　*

Barrie McDermott fits the description of classic 'minder'. He certainly was to me in my early days. From the start we had the makings of a strong friendship. If you spend 350 days a year travelling and playing with someone you'd better get on. You see the good, the bad and the ugly.

Barrie related well to the younger lads. He was funny and didn't mind being the butt of someone's joke. But to have a front-rower who was feared was invaluable. In the nine-year period when we travelled together he felt like a big brother to me. If someone hit me late or took liberties with me, Barrie was going to fix it up on my behalf.

You might want more detail on that. The game in those days was different to today's version; so, depending on the position, Baz would hit somebody particularly hard, perhaps in the face, particularly in the scrums. That was still going on back then. Baz was an especially aggressive ball carrier. If he ran straight at you, you had to front up. And running straight at someone who had hit me late earlier in the game would convey the message Baz was aiming to get across. He would provide that service to most of us. Kylie Leuluai was similarly adept at dishing out warnings – or revenge.

These giants sorted issues out for you without having to say anything, either to you or to the player being reprimanded.

I could look after myself. I should emphasise that. But I'm not a fighter in that sense of the word. In some ways rugby's values in those days were skewed. If you traded punches with someone it was seen as unacceptable. But hitting someone late – a cheap shot – was somehow less reprehensible.

At Castleford in a Challenge Cup game one day, Dean Sampson, the international prop who was their enforcer, was sent off for a high shot on me. That evening we'd arranged a night out in Wakefield. Dean happened to be out in Wakefield too. And over he came, with a few choice words about how unjust it was that he'd been dismissed, even though he had clocked me around the eyebrows.

Baz appeared. Dean disappeared. Gone.

Dean Sampson was a handy bloke, but Baz, because he'd had so many red cards, had a reputation for taking the game to the edge. Over the twenty years of my career, Baz would be in the top three hard men of that time. Most players would have him in their three.

It's impossible to overstate the value of a player who can't be dominated or intimidated. In Kylie Leuluai we signed a player who had many of Baz's fearsome attributes. Kylie wouldn't throw a punch but he could hit like no one had ever seen. When he hit them, they stayed hit.

As Super League evolved there was less of that

hand-to-hand combat. But Baz had grown up with it and kept it in his locker. He was ready for whatever physical challenge a game might throw at him. As a youngster he'd played against some really handy big men like Kelvin Skerrett and Kurt Sorensen. But the game changed, and Baz was able to change with it. He was powerful but quick over short distances. Many modern players don't have Baz's aggression in their game. If they did, these days they'd spend more time in disciplinary hearings than on the field.

When Rob fell ill, Baz was supportive straight away. I'd have expected nothing less of people who were as fond of Rob as I was. All through the challenges at various points they would appear alongside me in solidarity.

* * *

Jamie Peacock (JP) was never going to need cajoling into supporting the MND work. The man's a rock, in sport and life. Jamie was Great Britain captain when he joined the Rhinos in 2005. His Bradford Bulls had just beaten us in a Grand Final. Understandably there was talk about him taking over our captaincy. I sat down with Tony Smith, our head coach, and told him: 'If you make Jamie captain, I'll understand. I won't change. I get it.'

But Tony didn't make the switch, and from the first minute Jamie was great with me. He's the sort to go after problems and kick the door in. I'm more reflective. So in tandem we were ideal. Jamie spoke up a lot in meetings, set standards, sacrificed a lot. We'd bounce off each other in those meetings and in preparations for games. A very healthy relationship. The strength of our friendship took four or five years to fully mature. By then we knew each other inside out.

Without JP we wouldn't have continued to win trophies. 'He was from Bramley, but it was like he'd come from Sparta,' our team-mate Jamie Jones used to say about JP, who had a huge capacity to endure pain and darkness and just hold tight in those moments.

JP was a warrior for us. During the last season we spent together he was battered. He'd turn up on game night with his hair dyed black, looking a million dollars; then you saw him on a Monday and he'd come in as a grey-haired old man, bent over. Then he'd transform himself again, put the rinse through and look twenty-four once more. He was as tough as they come.

He used to shout: 'RIGHT, THIS LOT ARE 'AVIN IT!' It wouldn't have fitted my position or style of play to shout such words. But you needed someone to. And Jamie would say it and deliver on it every single week.

When we walked away from our Rhinos playing days on the same day in 2015 I felt physically well. I was fit. That had given me an edge in the game until the end – especially in the repeat efforts, the waves of ball carrying and tackling that drive both sides up and down the pitch. I had known I could stick in there – endure. My body was still intact. I hadn't had any major injuries. JP on the other hand had had an anterior cruciate ligament (ACL) injury and other operations. His race was run. But he's still tough, still running and doing challenges. Being three years younger than Jamie obviously also worked to my advantage. He was a front-line soldier, constantly getting whacked and whacking people in turn. He was always expected to be the most physical guy on the field.

Mentally, it was the right time for me to go. Mentally *and* physically, I'd say JP was cooked. But several times when the going got tough on the challenges, I felt his reassuring presence lift me.

* * *

Jamie Jones-Buchanan (JJB) is an intrinsic part of my life, now, as then. We're the same age and spent seven or eight years playing against each other, in Lancashire v. Yorkshire games, twice a season. He was Yorkshire's best player. We beat them heavily, pretty much every time, but he was always the ultra-competitor in their team. We'd played England schoolboys together and joined the Leeds academy around the same time. We travelled down the same track.

Like me, he comes from a working-class background. But as personalities we're polar opposites. I like routine. I'm methodical about how best to do things. Not a perfectionist, but someone who'd rather get it right first time rather than looping back to re-do it. Jamie forgets everything. Loses everything. But he is so creative. Funny, philosophical. Like JP, he comes from Bramley and liked to amuse himself by calling it 'the big apple'. He has a unique way of looking at life.

He was born with a twisted pelvis, so it's remarkable he could even run, never mind play rugby. Early in his career an abductor muscle ripped off his pelvis. Multiple surgeries followed and over the next eighteen months he rarely played. Adversity tried to trip him up all the way to the top, yet he's still the most competitive bloke I've met. If JP's determined and stubborn and headstrong, JJB will either fight you or burst into tears – both because he only wants to win. He once said: 'Even eating my dinner, I want to be the first to finish.' He has no arrogance about him, and no ego. He's good for me.

In all my best memories, Jamie is there or thereabouts. He has been someone for me to lean on in the bad moments. He's always been there. In 2015 when we won the Treble, Jamie injured his leg badly before the climax of the season ('my kneecap was down near my shin', he said) and was in a suit when we won the Challenge Cup. I asked him to come up the steps with me to collect the trophy. We took a handle each and raised it to the crowd – me in my filthy kit, Jamie in his suit.

* * *

The cast of my team-mates is strong; but of course a life in sport is shaped not only by your team-mates but by your bosses, the guys who pick the team and decide how you're going to play. Rob and I both had ups and downs with the men in charge of Leeds. Many more ups than downs. And by supporting each other through the downs I guess we were laying another foundation stone of our friendship.

The head coaches

Dean Bell would have been my second hero alongside Ellery. Soon after I joined Leeds at thirteen, Dean came in to replace Doug Laughton. He went out of his way to talk to me and gave me a book, *The Edge*, with a personal message. I'd often draw on its wisdom. Dean was a huge influence who gave me my first-team debut and then became my academy coach when he dropped down from first-team duties. As I studied for my A-levels and played most of my games for the academy I couldn't have asked for a better mentor. He was brilliant, disciplined, tough, and had that aura about him because he'd been there and done it, though he never rammed that down your throat. He wanted us to play the right way and had some wonderful values – the same ones I was brought up with.

Graham Murray came in as head coach when Dean stepped down and did a wonderful job of turning the team into a force again. Leeds made the inaugural Grand Final in

1998 and won the Challenge Cup in 1999. He was very strict, could be quite nasty at times in his delivery. A fair bit of the time he was fired-up. Graham went back to Australia in 2000 to coach the Sydney Roosters and was replaced at Headingley by **Dean Lance.**

I struggled under Dean, who treated the young players differently to the senior lads. Now I can understand the thinking behind the method – to show the youngsters what they needed to do to reach the top. But a memory sticks out of him sending a handful of the senior lads to a jacuzzi and spa at David Lloyd's while we were training ankle-deep in mud. I'm thinking: we're all in this together, aren't we? Why aren't we all going to David Lloyd's?

Dean is the coach who left me out of the Challenge Cup final in 2000 after I'd played every game that year. I lost a lot of respect for him that day. He got the bullet four matches into the following season (2001) and **Daryl Powell** took over. Now, I loved playing under Daryl. I had played along-side him for a couple of years and he had of course been my first room-mate – this seventeen-year-old kid rooming with a 35-year-old father figure. Daryl was close with Barrie McDermott and our former captain Iestyn Harris and made it his business to look after me. He didn't get the credit he deserved for the work he did at the time with the young lads. The time and effort he invested in us set the club up for a long time.

Tony Smith came in when Daryl elected to step down in

the summer of 2003. Tony was transformational too because he was able to take us from a team rich in 'potential' to a gang of winners. The perception was that Leeds had spent a load of money on star players who didn't deliver in big games. The young players inherited that tag but didn't have the baggage because we hadn't had those experiences. You could see there was a hungry young group coming through. The club had won academy titles for a decade but it hadn't quite kicked through yet to first-team success.

Tony was a very technical and tactical coach, challenging all the time. Our friendship endures.

Under Tony, we had two young players, Chev Walker and Ryan Bailey, sent down over a street fight. Prison visits and writing to team-mates behind bars was a new experience for me as captain. It rocked us.

Chev made his debut at sixteen, as I had. We played a World Cup together in 2000. He was aggressive in training and games but off the field was a good guy. 'Bails' was a rough diamond. You could imagine him getting into scuffles but he had a kind heart. Towards the back end of his time with Leeds he would regularly miss Mondays because he'd been at a Sunday club somewhere, which some of the lads would resent. But if you watch the sports documentary miniseries *The Last Dance*, and see Dennis Rodman's part in it, you know it happens in sport. Ryan was nonetheless one of the fittest players. I loved playing with him. When the message went up to get behind Rob, after he'd been diagnosed with MND, Ryan was straight on the phone and wanted to play. It meant a lot to him.

Social media was in its infancy then. Soon everybody had camera phones. Everyone wanted to tell a tale on a Leeds player on a night out. That meant we had a strict regime imposed on when we could go out, where, and who with. Away from the training ground we became very con-trolled. Some of the lads found it oppressive and struggled to adapt. I can see why the club took the stance it did but it wasn't easy to be so constrained in our social lives.

Tony Smith has mellowed since, but he could be severe in his video review sessions, tearing strips off people. I wasn't spared. To his credit he'd go after the older pros more than the younger players. That's preferable. Often it's the other way round.

Those truth and reconciliation sessions were long. On the menu of crimes would be positioning, handling errors, missed tackles, decision making. He'd rarely attack the per-son, more the behaviour. One of the worst things you can call a rugby team is soft. 'That was a soft performance.' I hate hearing that because it sends a shudder through me. At half-time, 'Boys, you've been soft' was an accusation that caused me every time to think: it's not because we're not tough enough.

But we were successful under Tony's harsh reign. Today you don't see so many brutally honest game reviews, where a player can be singled out in front of team-mates. It was an

intense captain–coach relationship. Most nights after training Tony would call me at home to talk more. You'd be
trying to do your bit with the kids and have to break off for
a forty-five-minute call with the coach. I knew it was a role
I had to play and it was my chance to get the dressing-room
view across to him. He didn't always like it, but it was best
coming from the captain.

Brian McClennan was Tony's opposite. Four years of Tony
made us successful but we were ready for a change of mood.
Brian was less picky and challenging on the minor details. It
was all big-picture stuff. A heart of gold, fun, laid back. I
hardly ever spoke to him on the phone. It was still a strong
captain–coach relationship but with a different dynamic.

Tony's demeanour was of the teacher in a classroom. And
of course our dressing room was full of lads who'd done
everything they could in childhood to escape the classroom. Brian revived the possibility that there was another
way to be successful, and he was very good at getting us up
for big games. A skilled motivator, who knew which emotional seeds to sow.

At the hotel in Manchester one Grand Final day, Brian
brought all the families – kids, wives, parents, grandparents –
into a meeting room at 3 p.m., ahead of the 6 p.m. kick-off.
We all wandered down to the room to find them there. And
they sang to us. They'd practised the song all the way from
Leeds to Manchester. It gripped you. You knew what you
were playing for, because it was there, right in front of you.

Brian McDermott was the best I had. For 99.9 per cent of the time we had the best captain–coach relationship anyone could have. He knew that if he gave us a gameplan I'd deliver it. He had a military background. He'd played the game and understood it, had a good manner. He'd fire up and get shitty, as most coaches would, and there would be some tetchy reviews, but I loved playing for him, even with what happened in 2015, when I found myself in the wilderness for a large part of the season. More on that in Chapter 6.

*　　*　　*

Naturally, success at Leeds led many of us to be regulars for England and Great Britain. Rob won fifteen caps for England and played five times for GB between 2004 and 2007. I played twenty-six games for England from 2000 to 2013 and fourteen matches in Great Britain colours. So we were brothers in arms at national level too.

International rugby

Up until the last couple of years of my international career I felt I'd underachieved in the England and Great Britain jerseys. I don't think I'd be alone in that feeling over the last fifty years. I appeared in the Ashes series of 2001 and 2003, and the 2005 Tri-Nations. Only four of those fourteen games produced Great Britain wins. The GB team was largely phased out from 2007.

When I arrived on the international scene the key guys going for the jersey I wanted were Andy Farrell, captain of the country, and Paul Sculthorpe, who was man of steel time after time. The two best players in the two best teams of the time, Wigan and St Helens. Not easy. I didn't have the size or athleticism those two had. They were bigger, better men. I had to find a way round those inconvenient realities and find a role for myself as the utility guy. I made my England debut as the hooker and played my second game at scrum-half.

I struggled to get any real foothold in the international game, which was significantly different to club rugby. British rugby league at that time was free-flowing, with a lot of offloads and ball movement. The Australian game on the other hand was more conservative: five straight hard carries and a kick downfield. I was more suited to the British style but in Test rugby we'd often try to play like the Aussies or Kiwis, which probably didn't suit my skill set. In a collision between a 6ft 18st guy and one who is 6ft 14st there's only going to be one winner most of the time. Those stones counted against me.

Enough chances came my way. But it was only in my final two years that it all clicked.

With England we had waves of strength and weakness. When I first joined, the national set-up was a Wigan clique and that was tricky. You could feel it in camp. The national team would have been improved by greater togetherness. Lots of national teams in different sports would diagnose the same problem. Pulling the various club elements together is arguably the number one skill of international coaching.

I played in the World Cups of 2000, 2008 and 2013. We arrived at the 2008 tournament after St Helens had beaten Leeds in the Challenge Cup semi-finals but we'd defeated them 24–16 in the Grand Final. The vast majority of the England camp was Leeds and Saints – thrown together two days after that Grand Final. Both sets of lads had been on the beer, then flown to Australia and placed on a drinking ban. That was a tough sequence to adapt to.

I supported the alcohol ban because I thought we were there to do a job. I wasn't even drinking, so it didn't affect me personally, but really we should have just gone out and broken down the Saints–Leeds grudges. There wasn't the unity you need for a successful World Cup campaign. We beat Papua New Guinea but then lost 52–4 to Australia and 36–24 to New Zealand. We couldn't carry on like that.

Steve McNamara was in charge of England from 2010 to 2015 and knocked down those barriers, much as Gareth Southgate did with the football team. We had to come together or keep reaching the same dead end.

Towards the end of my thirteen years with England I felt Steve really wanted me in the team, in my club role, so I no longer felt like the utility man. Steve gave me the confidence to bring my club game to international rugby and I played my best stuff under his management.

When I look back at the 2013 World Cup, how close we were still hurts. One of my favourite memories is of winning the 2012 Grand Final against Warrington, having been smacked all over the place by them six weeks earlier in the Challenge Cup final, then taking a call the next day from Steve to be told I would be England captain for the 2013 tournament.

Wins over Ireland and Fiji earned us a quarter-final place. There we beat France 34–6 and progressed to a semi at Wembley against New Zealand. But that game, in which Rob was on the bench, was agony. We were seconds away from the final when Shaun Johnson broke away to score a converted try to give the Kiwis a 20–18 win. There was no time to hit back. It was no consolation to have played probably my best game in an England shirt.

The pain of defeat left me talking to Steve on the coach home about international retirement. He asked me not to decide in haste. I desperately wanted another go at it – wanted to play in a World Cup final. In reality I'd played my last game for my country. I returned to Leeds where, two years later, there would be a happier ending to my club career, with Rob and the lads.

6

THE MIRACLE OF 2015

My final season as a Leeds Rhino was an unusual mix of wretched and wonderful. It was a year when my career threatened to end in bitterness but which instead carried me to a miraculous treble of trophies.

I spent my whole rugby league career at Leeds Rhinos because I was always content there and felt looked after. There was never any doubt in my mind that this was a special club. Loyalty matters to me. Fulfilment was more important than fame. If I'd left Headingley to go somewhere else for more money then everything I'd always said about the values of the team wouldn't have meant anything any more.

I was happy with my lot. There wasn't another league club in the UK I would have considered joining. Unlike many clubs, Leeds had a decent bonus structure. Their philosophy was: we'll reward success. And we made sure we had the success to trigger the bonuses, so both sides won – the team and the club.

I felt a loyalty too to the Leeds supporters. I was playing with my best mate, Jamie, and another four or five who were close friends, including Rob. We were the best-supported club in England. There were so many reasons to be appreciative of the life I had. Family stability was top of that list. Had I moved around our family life might have looked quite different.

And yet my final year at Headingley was turbulent. It wasn't the romantic swansong a scriptwriter would have set out for a 34-year-old leaving a club he had joined as a child.

Part of the background is that I'd always wanted to play rugby union. At the end of 2002 I met the England head coach Clive Woodward to discuss the possibility of switching to union but decided against it. I felt I needed to win trophies in league before embarking on that fresh adventure. I don't regret saying no to Clive.

The following year his team won the 2003 World Cup, in Australia, but I wouldn't have made that squad. I'd have been too raw. There's no reason to think I missed out on a union World Cup winner's medal. The switch would have been more geared to the following World Cup in 2007, when England reached the final but lost to South Africa.

The discussion with Woodward was about me playing inside centre initially and then perhaps no. 10 further down the track. At that time my physique was more suited to playing in the no. 12 position, the closer of the two centres to the fly-half. In league I was a ball-carrying loose forward who had an offload and broke the gain-line. Towards the end I found myself in a very different role. I barely broke the line at all but still had an offload. I was a game manager.

At the time the Rugby Football Union were targeting league players. Financially I'd have been far better off. But I felt it was the wrong time. I needed to win something at Leeds. Within a couple of months I'd re-signed there and they'd made me captain.

Rugby union didn't enter the picture again for more than a decade. A couple of offers came my way to play in the NRL in Australia but the Leeds CEO, Gary Hetherington, was shrewd in his handling of our core group. Gary would encourage you to sign a long-term deal. And when you'd done so he would sit you down at the end of every year and add a few more pennies and another year to your contract. Before you knew it, you were thirty with a five-year commitment. Then, the opportunities to move started to dry up – because nobody wanted to pay a transfer fee.

Although I was glad I'd been a one-club man at Leeds, by 2015 there was one small cloud of doubt. I'd be finishing my playing career with no other experiences to test me and look back on in later life. In 2008 I'd graduated from Leeds Beckett University with a BSc (Hons) in Sport and Exercise Science. Seven years later at the same institution I added an MA Sport Business degree. I'd always felt I ought to be in fresh environments to expand my knowledge. On the playing side, I'd been asked a number of times to go over and play union with Leeds Carnegie, and it was always in my mind to play a season or two at the back end of my league career. Carnegie emerged as the obvious place to satisfy that urge.

Winning the Challenge Cup in 2014 was pivotal because, as I mentioned earlier, I'd lost five as Leeds captain. To finally win one completed my collection of domestic honours. From there it was easier to think clearly about giving union a go. The deal was done in January 2015. We then started the 2015 season at Rhinos with a really good squad – as good as I can remember – and lots of talented young lads coming through.

But six or eight weeks into the season I found myself on the bench and starting to feel squeezed. By this stage it had been announced that I was moving across to rugby union at the end of the summer.

My role in the Rhinos team had already changed. My body type had altered, I was less of a power player and more of a game manager who could repeat effort after effort after effort. Every three or four years in a long rugby career you need to tweak what you are about. From when I started to when I finished, rugby league had evolved into a very different game. My job was to control the team and get us round the pitch. The special, creative or try-scoring moments I'd had early in my career were now largely memories.

I found myself out of the team, found myself being

Rugby has given me some of the best things I have in my life. It's not just about the game itself. It's about community and friendship.

Here with mum and dad. They never really wanted three kids. I remind them of this and tell them regularly – I was the best mistake you ever made.

Rugby hooked me quickly. By ten I knew there was more to it than just enjoying the game.

I signed professionally with Leeds Rhinos at thirteen and made my debut at sixteen.

Jayne and I met when I was twenty on a night out in Oldham. Without her I couldn't have done any of this. I couldn't have hoped for a better wife, companion or friend.

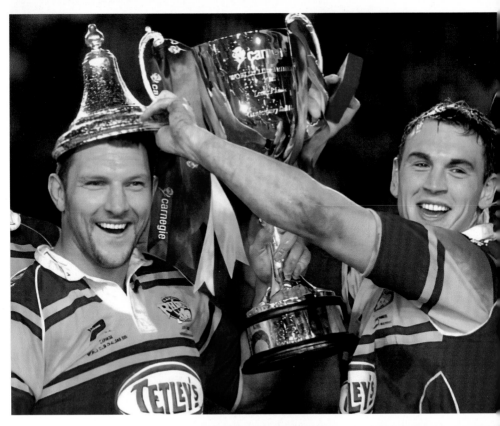

Barrie McDermott has always felt like a big brother to me. If someone hit me late or took liberties with me, Barrie was always going to fix it up on my behalf.

In all my best memories, Jamie Jones-Buchanan (JJB) has been there.

Me playing against London Broncos in 2004.

My final game in an England shirt against New Zealand in 2013.

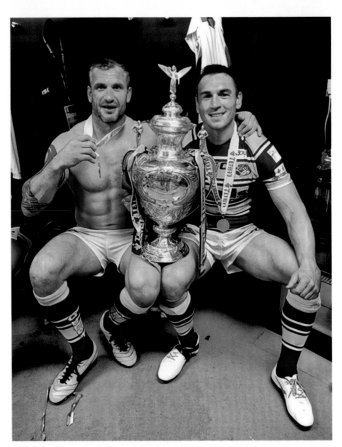

Jamie Peacock has been a rock, in sport and life. Just like at Rhinos, when the going got tough during the challenges, he'd lift me up.

Me, Jayne, Jack and Sam.

My seventh and last Grand Final game.
A 22–20 win against Wigan.

Celebrating with my seventh and last
Grand Final trophy.

Me and Jamie Jones-Buchanan lifting the Challenge Cup in 2015. JJB had injured his leg, but I still made him come with me to lift the cup in his suit.

The last game of my Rhinos career, the 2015 Grand Final at Old Trafford. The perfect goodbye. After all the doubt about whether I'd ever be picked again, that win allowed me to close the book.

dropped, which caused me great distress. The announcement about my move had already been made. Not only
that, but Leeds Carnegie wanted me to go early. I was sat
there at thirty-four thinking: if you don't want to play me, I
might as well go now.

There were some strained conversations.

One Friday before we played Widnes on the Sunday, we
were having a late training session. Shortly before that I'd
played my 500th game for the club. We'd faced Warrington
and I'd been put on the bench. My kids were mascots. We
were getting beat by thirty or forty points when I was sent
on for the last ten minutes. A lot of people said to me after
the game: it was massively disrespectful to use you in that
way.

My reflex reply was: oh no, it's part of the game, I understand my role, I've got to fight to get back in, and so on. But
it upset a lot of people who were close to me.

We move on to the next Friday team meeting and the
starting side is announced. I'm not in it. I'd been on the
bench the week before but now I have no part in it
whatsoever.

We step on to the field to train, and I feel seventeen or
eighteen again – those years when you're on the fringe, and
you're looking for every movement, listening to every conversation the head coach is having to see where you stand.
Four different players are called over, and I think: they're
his bench.

I'm the fifth to be summoned. I'm told that I'm not in the team, not needed, not needed the week after for a cup game at home against Huddersfield. I may be needed at Hull KR away the week after that, but it would depend how the team functioned between now and then.

So I say to our head coach Brian McDermott, 'What do you want me to do?'

Brian shrugs his shoulders and says, 'I don't care.'

No eye contact.

I knew I was done. That was it. This was the ending to my wonderful time with Leeds.

I was determined that rugby wasn't going to define my life. It had given me all these fabulous things but I wasn't going to spend the next forty years looking back on it. I wanted something else, something new. But right from the start that year I knew we had a chance of winning trophies. I didn't think we'd win the Treble, but trophies, yes. A good send-off was on the cards. The chances were I was going to leave on a high.

At the end of the training session where I was called over as the fifth man, the lads were given the Saturday off. I came in on the Saturday morning and ran with some of the eighteen- and nineteen-year-olds, which was beneficial for all of us, because the youngsters were seeing that Kevin Sinfield could get dropped. They'd never witnessed that before, and quickly understood that I was shoulder to shoulder with them.

The conditioning department stayed tight with me and promised whatever help I needed to keep myself sharp.

That Sunday, my son Jack, who was ten, was playing away in St Helens, against a team called Clockface. My plan was to watch Jack play, then tell him to pick a mate to bring to the Widnes–Leeds game, which would be only five minutes away.

Eighty minutes before kick-off, in the stands, I told them I was just nipping down to the dressing room. As I walked in, I made eye contact with Brian – who I get on brilliantly with now. If looks could kill from a head coach, I'd have dropped down dead.

Friday – he didn't care.

Sunday – I get that look.

The writing's on the wall.

I wasn't daft enough to think this could be rectified. I didn't feel welcome. Somehow I'd gone from this being 'our' dressing room to it being a place that didn't involve me.

I walked round, shook everybody's hand and left. I was in there for forty seconds, then back in the stands. I sat there and paid no attention whatsoever to the game. Jack on the other hand was quite excited. He couldn't have known what I was feeling. It was a lacklustre, tired performance. We lost by fifty.

On Monday we were all back in for training. Recovery, swimming, review – for those who'd played. Non-players: conditioning.

I made my way on to the training field. Opposite the pitch, Brian's window opened and a voice called through it: 'Kev, have you got a minute?'

I ran back in and took my boots off.

'How are you?'

'I'm all right.'

'No, how are you?'

'It is what it is. I'm all right.'

'We might need you this week.'

And that was it. I was back in.

In the 2018 Leeds Rhinos film *As Good as It Gets?* Brian denied that his handling of me was reverse psychology: 'It wasn't a mad strategy by me . . . Kev wasn't playing well enough to get the shirt.' Naturally I dispute that.

We played Huddersfield at home in a quarter-final, on the BBC. A lot of the build-up was about me being left out the previous week. I was voted man of the match.

Back home, I sat down and worked out how many games I had left, how many training sessions, counting down the days to a possible Grand Final. When I reflect now, it was such a sad way to finish.

I'm going to be frank. My mindset was: I'm going to ram this down your throat and you'll never question me or my position in this team again. We can laugh and joke about it now. Brian's word for me was 'stubborn'. Yeah, I'm stubborn – I'd like to think stubborn for the right reasons. When I'm wrong I'm happy to admit it. But if I'm put in an unfair or difficult situation, I'm going to fight.

Ultimately I suspect I was being punished for agreeing to join Carnegie. Not that I said so at the time, because I didn't want to unsettle the team by making it political. The player who took my spot, Liam Sutcliffe, was a seriously talented young guy, and I said to him at the time: this isn't about you and me, there's room for both of us in this team. I told him: there are things you can do better than me, stuff I can't do any more. But I also knew that when it came to big games, that's where I had the edge. Nobody had my game management or calmness in big moments. That's how I knew there was still a role for me.

I couldn't make a 60-yard break any more or chip the full-back, but I could deliver a gameplan and make sure we got the team round the field the way it needed to move. Pressed to explain his reasoning, Brian might well have said my form wasn't good enough. My counter-argument would have been that he underestimated the value of me getting round the team and making it function. I always felt I could get more out of those around me – get them from a six to a seven or eight out of ten.

At the end of August we won the Challenge Cup, with me and Jamie Jones raising the trophy together (as I mentioned earlier, him in his suit) after a dominant 50–0 win over Hull KR.

The League Leaders' Shield was a good deal harder to win. The game that clinched it is secure in rugby league legend. The *Guardian* called it the sport's Sergio Agüero moment. We were playing Huddersfield at the John Smith's Stadium in late September. We'd lost three in a row after the Challenge Cup final. Two minutes from time I kicked a penalty that drew us level. The Shield was seemingly heading to Wigan, who beat Castleford to put themselves in prime position.

People wondered: why had I taken the kick when we so desperately needed to win? Even some of my team-mates were nonplussed. My decision can be traced to an old wound: the 2003 Challenge Cup final, in my first year as captain.

With a couple of minutes to go that day we were two points behind when we were awarded a penalty. I chose not to kick for goal. We tapped the ball and went for the big score against Bradford, who were the best team that year. In a replay they would have beaten us. So we went for the win, in the here and now. After three tackles we kicked the ball dead – wasted it. I'd always believed that if we'd played the full set we'd have scored. Bradford were all hands on hips, doubled over. We had 'em. But we lost 22–20. The blame fell on me – and it stuck. For years afterwards people asked me whether I should have taken that kick. People can be brutal in their judgements. The whole experience hardened me for the next twelve years as captain.

So the decision I took at Huddersfield a dozen years later

was based entirely on winning the game. The play-off permutations were clear in my head. I knew that by drawing the match we'd put the trophy in a helicopter to Wigan for them to collect. I just believed we had enough still in us to go and win. The experience and resilience I'd acquired from 2003 came to my assistance when the same dilemma arose in 2015.

From childhood rugby on, anxiety never undermined me in big decision-making moments. I always knew that if I got those choices wrong it would be for the right reasons. When a decision was the wrong one it was usually because my feel for that particular game wasn't as good as it usually was. My goal kicking was reliable, which helped. It might have been different had I made the decisions and then handed the ball to someone else to kick. And remember, I had strong people around me to support my choices.

We attacked again from the restart and Danny McGuire had something special in mind. He chipped ahead with beautiful precision and the ball bounced up into the arms of Ryan Hall, who steamed down the touchline for the try. Danny didn't chip ahead like that very often but was known for cooking up game-changing moments. So was Rob. You could say we had a lucky bounce. Or you could emphasise the incredible skill from Danny and Ryan.

In the replays you can see the euphoria sweeping through us – and our fans. It was the excitement you get when the impossible becomes reality.

Throughout my time at Leeds I knew we had an unbe-lievably relentless team who would work for each other. Often you would go down the opposition team list and say St Helens, for example, are better than us. But as soon as the rain started or it became a tactical battle I knew we would win – in part because I knew we'd kick better than they could.

We were blessed with a lot of players who refused to lose, or refused to give in. I wish we could have found an easier way of doing it, but we had to be on the ropes in games to be able to say: 'Right, we've created enough of a black hole for ourselves, created enough crap around us, let's show everybody we can fight our way out of it.' We didn't talk about it that way but it was how it needed to be for us. We would make it as dark as we could for ourselves. Subcon-sciously that brought out the best in us.

From the wilderness, I now had the chance to leave with a Treble and a last Grand Final win, to wear that jersey one last time in a season-defining game: Leeds Rhinos v. Wigan Warriors at Old Trafford on 10 October 2015. Me, Jamie Peacock and Kylie Leuluai were all bowing out. Kylie had been a great support to me during my time in the doghouse. Jamie too, though nothing could alter his mindset, which was: I'm getting this job done, and whoever's in my way is getting out of my way. In As Good as It Gets? JP spoke about the toll playing into his late thirties had taken on him. He said, 'You walk round in a lot of physical pain, six days a week.' But he wasn't going to go out quietly. For the three of us there would be one last game with Rob, who, as he said in his own book, was dreading the thought of so many of his old comrades leaving the club after the final whistle.

The Treble we were bearing down on – Challenge Cup, League Leaders' Shield and Super League Grand Final – had last been achieved by St Helens in 2006. We were without Stevie Ward, who had dislocated his shoulder in the semi-final win against Hull.

It was a typical final. Wigan were an excellent side. Cagey. We led 16–6 at half-time but went 20–16 behind in the third quarter. Then Josh Walters scored an equalising try for us and I put the ball down to kick my 1,792nd goal for Leeds. A 22–20 win – my seventh and last Grand Final trophy. I threw myself into the arms of Jamie Peacock, who reflected years later on what it had taken out of us to win on all three fronts: 'Everyone was spent. Emotionally empty.'

After all the doubt about whether I'd ever be picked again, that win allowed me to close the book. A book of wonderful highs and terrible lows. But I suppose that's what everyone's career would look like. I would return to Leeds as director of rugby – something we'd discussed as a possibility around the time of my final contract. But my days of pulling on that shirt were over. I know Rob felt bereft when the three of us left the club that day.

Watching the lads celebrate, I'd always feel so fulfilled and content. They'd be forever offering me a drink but usually I just wanted to savour it with no distortions. From then on rugby league wouldn't define me any more. There were no demons, no lingering regrets to haunt me.

On the way back from the final I sat next to Brian. He fist-pumped me on the arm, saying, 'Are we all right?'

We'd been so close as captain and coach until the rupture and those cold words in the middle of 2015. Now it was all about business, about winning trophies.

So I said, 'Yeah, I'm all right.'

'But are we really all right?' Brian said.

And I told him, 'Look, we both got what we wanted.'

7

PART OF THE UNION:
A YEAR AT CARNEGIE

There's a detail about my last Grand Final win that I neglected to mention. I performed in it with a broken hand that was to play a role in the timing of my next move.

After the Old Trafford match in October 2015, Leeds were to play New Zealand a fortnight later in a warm-up game for the tourists. But by then I was eager to get through the door at Carnegie, who'd splashed a lot of money on the squad and were hoping to gain promotion. Leeds Rhinos wouldn't let me join Carnegie until my contract was up at the end of November, so I was left twiddling my thumbs.

They'd asked me to play in the New Zealand game – and I'd have gladly turned out, even with a hand that was still broken. But I thought: if you're not going to let me go early, I'm not playing against an international side with a broken hand.

I've played in a play-off series with a fractured cheek-bone, and with a fractured eye socket. A broken hand was no barrier to me. There had to be give and take, though, and it wasn't forthcoming from Leeds' end.

We took a quick holiday, and if you ask me what was the best break I've been on, I would pick that one. It was the only time I felt fully content on holiday. I'd brought to a close something I'd been doing since the age of seven. That feeling lasted the whole time we were away.

The transition to Carnegie and rugby union was waiting up ahead and I had no idea how tough it would be. Especially the defending. I was constantly trying to run back 10 metres, as you have to in rugby league. It's such a hard habit to break. League is such a fast-flowing game. Now the rugby I was playing was stop-start and peppered with set pieces. Because it was the level below top flight there was a mix of full-time and part-time players. Some games were quick in good conditions against the better teams. In some, you were ankle-deep in mud.

I didn't mind that I was back playing in the cold, wind and rain. I didn't mind playing in front of two blokes and a dog. It was understanding the rules that gave me a problem. But I enjoyed the challenge, loved going into a new dressing room. Quite soon you realise that rugby lads are rugby lads, regardless of the code.

I went in on a similar salary to the one I had been on at Rhinos. But I stayed for just one season. About six weeks into my new start an adviser friend I had been working with sat me down and told me that the investment promised to

Carnegie to develop the squad would not be coming. That was in December 2015. I didn't fret. I was sure it would work out. In January, however, we met again and the same warning was conveyed.

Carnegie's position was that they wanted me to stay for the full two years and would honour my contract. At the same time they warned me that the quality of player I would be running out with in season two would drop substantially.

Meanwhile an enquiry came in from rugby league's governing body. Would I be interested in a job? The director of rugby role at Leeds Rhinos had gone quiet, so I met with the Rugby Football League performance director, Jon Roberts, who I had a lot of respect for. He asked me to go in a couple of days a week to work as rugby director. Later, after the 2017 World Cup, I took on the role of head of the England Performance Unit. I signed up in August 2016 and stayed until February 2020 when I left to concentrate on being director of rugby at Leeds Rhinos.

With the RFL job, events began to align. My rugby union career lasted just seven months but the parting was amicable. And I was coming out of my playing career unscathed, after nearly 600 games.

At Rhinos from 2018, my mission was to create a link between the head coach and chief executive. In all my time as captain that relationship was never as healthy as it ought to have been. There was something missing, a bridge that should have connected the two roles.

Gary Hetherington, our CEO, was very business-oriented. He wanted to dip into the rugby side – but only dip in. The head coach had thirty players to look after, on top of the full rugby department, recruitment and selection, with all the confrontational discussions that come with that job. It was too much. He needed the equivalent of the director of football role. My job was to oversee the relationships with the players and make sure the philosophy of the club was on track. That role had been mooted for me towards the end of my playing days. But the minute I agreed to go over to Carnegie I never heard that possibility mentioned again – until Brian McDermott was sacked.

The first six weeks of being an ex-player are blissful because you can make your own decisions. You're no longer institutionalised. Then you start to miss it – that routine. You miss being on a rugby field and feeling free. Many players will agree with me when I say that's where you feel most free. Nothing else professionally will replicate those feelings. If I could have played rugby until I was sixty-five, I probably would have done. In a media interview I admitted missing playing 'every single day'. And I'm aware of the contradiction with my earlier point about feeling liberated on holiday after I'd finished playing for Rhinos. It's just that the sense of being released doesn't last.

It didn't show, because I was always careful to line up new challenges, but for a while I felt lost. I could fill the time easily enough because there was plenty for me to do. It was

98

the fulfilment of playing that was taken away. That's where running came to my rescue.

As my playing career wound down I realised I was starting to envy people who took on big physical challenges. They became more and more appealing. Chris Stephenson, the CEO at Canterbury, my sponsor at the time, had once invited me to a State of Origin game in Australia, but I hadn't been able to go. The invitation was made again when I stopped playing.

It was on that trip that I fell in love with running. We jogged along the river in Brisbane, early, in the sunshine. The same again in Sydney, where we ran round the famous sites, stopping for photos. We went out every day for eight days. The only downside was that I hurt my foot, which meant I had to turn down an impromptu invitation to play for Sydney Roosters. I'd addressed them as a guest speaker and would have been tempted to try my luck, but my foot was in no condition for me to give it a go.

By the time I left Australia running was fixed in my mind as part of my future. I didn't run at school, didn't do cross country – it just wasn't part of my repertoire. I still don't classify myself as a runner. But straight away I started to feel the benefit mentally. Marathons and charity challenges were always in my thoughts because I felt I could use my profile from rugby to try to help and influence others.

The first marathon I signed up to was with Chris, for prostate cancer. Nobody knew, but my dad had been diagnosed with it. I'd heard the news after my last game for England. Soon I developed the urge to run two marathons a year, in April and October. It would stop me getting a belly, keep me in shape and maintain my mental health.

My spell at Carnegie established a connection that was later to play a major part in my work with Rob after his MND diagnosis. The Carnegie coach was the former Scotland scrum-half Bryan Redpath: big personality, likeable chap. We got on famously. When Rob was diagnosed, Bryan was on the phone within hours to offer support and suggest a meeting that turned out to be pivotal in many lives. That was where Doddie Weir came in . . .

8

DIAGNOSIS

It's our end-of-season dinner. First-team presentation night. We're all there: players, partners, sponsors, directors, staff. As academy head coach, Rob stands to announce our academy player of the year.

Jayne is with me. So is our head of performance, Jason Davidson. As soon as Rob starts speaking I look across to Jayne and she looks at me. I turn my eyes to Jason and he too is looking straight back at me.

I say to Jayne: he's drunk.

I'm Rob's boss now, as well as his friend, so there are several layers of concern from my side.

Rob returns to his seat. Another award is being handed out.

I make my way over to him, lean into him and say: 'Are you drunk?'

He looks at me. 'No.'

'Are you sure?'

'Yeah.'

'Have you taken anything?' (At that time he was suffering with shoulder pain from an old injury.)

'What do you mean?'

He's quite offended.

'Mate, you just spoke up there and you sounded drunk, you sounded terrible. What's going on?'

Rob says, 'Nothing. I promise you. I'm just really nervous.'

I return to sit next to Jayne and tell her, 'It must be the painkillers for his shoulder.'

Leading into that dinner, I'd noticed there was something not right in Rob's demeanour. But it was only at the awards ceremony where I saw it clearly. Something was seriously amiss.

Over the following fortnight I kept an eye on him at the training ground. He seemed much better. Two weeks after I'd challenged him, the academy players gathered for their own awards night. The winner already knew he'd won because his name had been announced at the main club dinner two weeks earlier, but they were going through it again so all the academy players and parents could be there this time.

As we're walking in, Rob and me, I say, joking, 'You've not had ten pints tonight have you?'

'Don't, Kev. Don't. You'll make me nervous.'

He gets up to speak. This time Jayne isn't here.

Same again. His speech is slurry. There are some words he can't say.

A few times before speech deserted him completely, in the thick of his illness, he couldn't say 'solicitor'. 'Necessity'. Things with an 's' in them. He would also later admit that when they were on holiday that August, Lindsey and his mum and dad had all said: what's going on with your voice? But at those two awards dinners, I didn't know any of it.

For the second time in a fortnight he's up on his feet making a speech that sounds all wrong.

I think: right. And I go over to him again.

'Are you in tomorrow?'

'Yeah.'

'Can I have half an hour?'

The next day he came in and sat in front of me.

I said, 'Look, what's going on? I'm worried about you.'

Rob insisted he was fine. I asked him about his shoulder. He said he was struggling with it. I asked him whether he was on painkillers.

'A few, but it's not what you think.'

So I told him, 'Let's get it checked out. Let's get your shoulder looked at. See the doc. And your speech as well?'

'No, no,' Rob said. 'There's nothing wrong.'

I stood my ground. 'But I'm going to mention it to the doc. Get it checked.'

The next port of call was our head of welfare, Nigel O'Flaherty Johnston. I asked Nigel to spend some time with

Rob to get him to open up in a way I couldn't. 'Try to find out what's going on.' Medical confidentiality came into play, but nevertheless I told Nigel: if there's anything more I need to do, you have to let me know.

That was mid- to late September 2019.

Rob was in great hands now. Nigel was a good, caring man. The first piece of news he brought me was encouraging: he said he didn't think it was drink or painkillers. At the same time I'd expressed my concern to our club doctor about Rob's shoulder and his speech. The response was that both should be examined. That sent Rob down a three-month path of tests.

In the early days of the testing Rob confided to me that he'd been doing all the Google searching people do when they're worried about their health. He'd confronted a doctor: 'Is it MND?' By that stage Rob was starting to succumb to slurring (dysarthria) and twitching. No wonder he was looking for answers on Google. Day by day he was inching towards the shock of his life. The test that confirmed the worst was one they conduct with an electric pulse through the body that returns a particular signal or ratio.

In the middle of December I'd been asked whether I'd be prepared to join Gareth Thomas in biking the Sports Personality of the Year trophy from Cardiff to Aberdeen. The idea was that I would do a leg of it in Scotland. A car collected me to take me to Gretna Green. It was the day Rob was in for a 5.30 p.m. appointment to be given his diagnosis, good or bad.

Only two weeks earlier Rob had been at a dinner in Cumbria with Danny McGuire. Danny had said, 'He's not right.' Perhaps I should have queried it with Rob and asked, 'Are you sure you want to go and do this dinner?' Danny reported news that felt familiar: people at the Cumbria dinner thought Rob was drunk.

I was getting picked up from home at seven. Time wore on. It was eating away at me. At 6.30 p.m. I chased Rob for news, by text.

The reply: 'I've got MND. It's been confirmed.'

I didn't understand much about MND then, but I knew one thing: it was a death sentence.

9

FIGHTING BACK WITH ROB

The car arrived on time at 7 p.m. for the drive to Gretna Green. The driver was a nice man who was keen to chat – heavy Manchester accent, big football fan, knew a bit about rugby league. But I was in no state to be nattering to anyone. All I could think about on that journey to Scotland was Rob and his family. Now it wasn't Rob on Google, it was me, in the back of that car, on the MND Association website, trying to understand more. I just stared at the alarming statistics glowing on the screen of my phone.

The world's come crashing down. I don't know exactly what this means, but I know it's horrendous.

A 50 per cent chance of living for two years.

A third die in the first twelve months.

At any one time 5,000 adults in the UK will have MND. Each day six people will die from it. It can affect people of any age but is more common in those over fifty.

MND is a fatal disease that affects the brain and spinal

cord. Muscles stop working when the nerves are under-mined. Sight, sound and feeling are usually unaffected. Around 35 per cent of sufferers experience mild cognitive deterioration. The association's telling me the disease can 'leave people locked in a failing body, unable to move, talk, swallow and eventually breathe'. Average life expectancy is between six months and three years from the onset of symptoms.

I was alone in that car with the shock of Rob's text. It wasn't my job to tell anyone else. I really wanted someone to talk to but I thought: it's not for me to share this. Over the next twenty-four hours Rob notified his closest friends but his initial feeling was that he didn't want to tell people outside the circle.

Prior to Rob's diagnosis I'd been aware of the disease because of Doddie Weir, and Joost van der Westhuizen, the South Africa scrum-half who died from MND in 2017. Sam Burgess's dad also died of MND when Sam was only fifteen. I played alongside Sam with Great Britain and Eng-land. I was also aware that Sam had struck up a friendship with the Nottinghamshire and England cricketer Stuart Broad, whose stepmother took her own life to escape MND, according to an inquest into her death. Sam and I had only short bursts together at international level and he didn't talk about it much. But I always knew it was there in the background.

I made it to Gretna Green, my mind still fogged. Next

morning we were up early, on a four-man bike. I was so glad to be at the back. Gareth was at the front with a *Blue Peter* presenter. I hardly spoke. Halfway through we pulled up for some refreshments and were chatting.

'Is everything all right?' Gareth asked.

'Yeah. I've just had a bit of bad news.'

Sooner than I expected, Rob decided he wanted to break the news. Now things moved fast, from an announcement to a press conference, and Rob being upset and struggling to get the words out. Even now the memory of that media event is guaranteed to make me well up – the sight of him, with us there, but also deeply alone, in some horrible sense.

A press release had gone out conveying the basic information. Now, Rob was down to do three or four one-to-one interviews to camera. One was with the BBC's Tanya Arnold, who has always been close to the rugby league family and particularly connected to Leeds. Because Rob knew her there was probably more emotion in their conversation. The TV spotlights were strong too, so even the room contained an emotional intensity. Tanya had been quite rocked by the news, and was sensitive with her questions, but it was inevitable that at some stage Rob would break down.

The question that did it was one about the effect it was having on his family. A fair question, but it broke Rob's defences.

It was in those moments when Rob disintegrated that you weren't completely sure what to do – step in, or give him space? I felt I needed to help break the interview up for him and give him time to gather his thoughts. So I stepped over and gave him a cuddle. It wasn't one of those cuddles where you're able to say 'It's going to be all right', because clearly it wouldn't be, just one of those hugs that say 'I'm here with you and I'll stand and fight with you.' I told him to take deep breaths, and how well he had done, how proud everybody was of him doing what he was doing.

It would have been easy for him to disappear and shy away, not let people in or understand what he was feeling and going through. We already knew Rob was courageous, but that day I saw a different side to him. I never imagined he'd be able to share publicly something so private. It wasn't the fight in him that took me unawares because I expected that. It was that such a private man was now addressing the world with the most deeply personal revelation anyone could imagine.

After those interviews we mingled for a while to take stock and make sure he was going to be all right. Which sounds absurd. How was he going to be all right? He wasn't.

The biggest thing I could give him at that point was my time and my support. I had this urge to go home with him and sit and talk to him about it, but by then it had been a turbulent day for him. He was bound to be exhausted.

Over the coming months, when he began to deteriorate, he was determined to show the outside world what it meant to have MND, and why we needed to fight the disease.

Some of this resolve to be open reflected Doddie Weir's influence.

Two or three days after Rob had announced he had MND, he and I drove to Carlisle to meet Doddie, my former Carnegie coach Bryan Redpath and Gary Armstrong, the former Scotland international who was doing a lot of driving for Doddie. We gathered at a Holiday Inn in Carlisle.

I knew Doddie by reputation from his playing days but hadn't met him. Bryan was like Rob: stocky, scrum-half, but full of chat, funny. We were so grateful that he reached out. Doddie talked to Rob. About the journey. What to expect. He talked a lot about sticking two fingers up to MND, not letting it win. He spoke about the postman, the fireman, the builder who didn't have the support he had, didn't have a rugby community to get behind him.

Doddie said, 'I'm here, you've got my number, I'm right behind you, I'll help in any way I can.'

He also brought various bits of kit to show Rob: devices that helped him eat, sit on chairs properly, an adapted pint glass that helped him drink. He was brilliant and funny with it.

That first meeting where Doddie spoke about the postman, the fireman and the builder resonated with Rob. It encouraged him not to live his life behind a door. He could see the opportunity to hit it head on. He knew rugby had given him a platform and that sharing his experience would

send a powerful message. When you see a 5ft 4in guy standing up to a calamity, it feels different somehow. It shouldn't,
but it does. It's like a little brother coming out and sharing
the most horrific news.

It was on the drive back from Carlisle that Rob opened
up about Lindsey and his mum and dad challenging him
months earlier about his voice.

We ran through some of the things Doddie had said, the
elements that stood out for Rob. It was easy to see: he was
worried about his kids.

He was grateful to me for the trip to see Doddie, but I
couldn't leave it there. I was doing what anyone would have
done. Just trying to help. And chance had played a role.
Without those last few months in rugby union at Leeds
Carnegie I wouldn't have known Bryan Redpath.

As I've said, on the subject of captaincy, one of my methods was to put myself in other people's shoes and consider
how it felt for them. Through that process I was starting to
ask myself: if this were me, in Rob's position, what would I
really want, what would help me on this journey?

For Rob, it was about the kids and Lindsey. That's what
started the conversation – one of the starkest but most
necessary you could ever have.

I said, 'We'll raise some money. How much do you need?'

Rob replied, 'No, I don't need anything. We're all right.
Lindsey works. We'll be all right.'

So proud.

'No. What do you need?'

I knew we could work out what Rob would need, what his current financial health was, and come up with a figure.

I came up with one.

And he burst into tears.

We're driving back from Carlisle, it's December, rolling it down, the windscreen wipers are on full, he's crying, I'm crying, I'm trying to drive . . .

* * *

Why did I feel this guiding urge to step in?

Because I was his captain.

Because I was his boss at the time, though I never felt like it. More like his older brother.

The first idea we had that December was to pull together a committee. About eight of us – right, what can we do? We knew we needed something to give us a big influx of funds, because I did say to Rob on that car journey: by next Christmas I'll make sure we've hit that target. I know I put my balls on the line but I didn't think it would be that hard. I didn't know Covid was coming. It was a hell of a lot of money but I knew how the rugby world would come together.

The first step was a big gala dinner at Headingley. A few favours were called in, from different sports, especially in Leeds. Jamie Jones's second testimonial game, for twenty years' service, was approaching. The match would be against

Bradford. I'd missed the chance to finish playing with Jamie on our terms because of an injury he'd sustained the year I finished. We had the picture of us holding the 2015 Challenge Cup trophy, and if you ask him about his favourite memory he'll say that Challenge Cup win because it symbolised our team and how we looked after one another.

In my mind I planned to come out of retirement and have ten minutes in Jamie's testimonial so we could have that ending together on the pitch. But it was Jayne's fortieth that year and she had grand plans for it.

I said, 'Look, on your birthday, Jamie's got his testimonial game that day and I'd quite like to play in it.'

She understood.

I whispered in the media manager Phil Daly's ear, 'If this game goes ahead I'll come on for the last ten minutes, only to finish the game with Jamie.'

Then we discussed the fact that a Leeds–Bradford game might attract 8,000 or so. I rang Jamie and asked, 'How would you feel about sharing your testimonial?' A rugby league testimonial is a big thing for a player. I told him, 'I think we can fill the ground.'

Jamie's reply: 'Yeah, I don't care whether we fill it or not. I'm in.'

As soon as he said that, I decided to play, and get some of the other ex-players to take part. The day was pieced together. Sky wanted to show it – they would never normally televise a game like that – and the BBC had developed a connection with Rob because of the interview he'd done with them about having MND, which told the story to the world.

I rang round the old boys. Jamie Peacock was in the initial meeting. So was Barrie McDermott, who couldn't play because his shoulder was knackered. Then some old Bradford boys came back for their team.

The game was a sell-out.

I was on the field for ten minutes. I wouldn't go so far as to say I 'played', but I was out there. Rob played too – came on for the last two minutes. And touched the ball. Slurred speech and a husky voice couldn't keep him off that field.

Before the game they'd put the old boys in a room together. Me, Jamie Jones, Jamie Peacock, Danny McGuire, Keith Senior, Ryan Bailey, Rob and Brett Delaney. We could have put another 100 players out there, that many people contacted me. But the league put a limit on the number of players we could use. The hour and a half in the dressing room before we took to the field was a brilliant exercise in rolling back the years. We were at the heart of it once more, transported five or ten years back into a special time. The banter was flying. Rob was getting it. He loved it. To raise so much money, for Rob to get out there on the pitch, for his kids to be mascots, for Jamie Jones to have such a testimonial after twenty years: the whole thing epitomised that group of people, the closeness, what the club represented.

I still ask myself: what is a club, what does it mean, what's it for? To me, it was that playing group.

Jayne's fortieth was still there waiting to be properly celebrated. She'd had a couple of days away planned, but had to accept me saying, 'You might just need to hang fire with that.' I thought a lot about how unselfish she had been, and all the times she'd worked around my career. She wouldn't have changed the day we combined Jamie's testimonial with Rob's fund-raiser. Our whole family was there to be part of it. A few weeks later Jayne did get the birthday trip she had planned.

The Headingley game gave the fund-raising the lift-off it needed. Soon after we staged the big gala dinner where the boxer Josh Warrington, Tracey Neville, Gareth Southgate, Will Greenwood and Kenny Logan were among the guests. There were so many different and distinguished sportspeople in the room. Leeds United sent a load of items for us to auction. Yorkshire County Cricket Club too. Teams from around the UK sent memorabilia. It was probably the biggest and best fund-raiser ever held at the club.

Then, in March 2020, Covid descended. I was due to run the Manchester Marathon for Rob in April. That got cancelled. So I ran round my local area, Saddleworth, instead. I didn't make a song and dance of it. But we raised five grand. It all adds up.

Then everything stopped.

*　*　*

I'd promised Rob that by Christmas morning in 2020, when his kids opened their presents, he would have the amount of money we'd discussed and be able to watch them tear off the wrapping paper with no financial worries. It was a good motivating image for all of us. But we reached September of that year and were short. The thought nagged me: I wanted to wake up on Christmas morning knowing Rob would be smiling inside. I was going to have to do something to close the gap.

Over the months there were numerous initiatives to keep the donations flowing. You could buy a share in a racehorse named after Rob – Burrow Seven, which made its debut at Catterick in December 2021, with Rob present. The former referee Dave Merrick would swim a mile every day for two months. There was an extraordinary surge in people coming up with ideas and putting them into practice. But what could I do next that would be distinctive and push the figures way above a few thousand pounds? As Rob's shirt number, 7, was always in our calculations, we came up with this figure of £77,777. I'd have taken on the next challenge for ten grand, but now we were aiming higher.

I told Jayne, 'I need to do something new for him.' My thoughts were still revolving around Rob's shirt number. 'I'm thinking seven marathons in seven days.'

Jayne's understandable response was, 'Are you mad?'

10

SEVEN MARATHONS FOR OUR NO. 7

I'd been bouncing ideas off Jayne for a while until seven marathons on seven consecutive days felt like the answer. As I said, she was sensibly sceptical. But on some level she knew it would be good for me to take it to that level. She knew it was what I needed to do.

This might make people sit up and notice, I said to myself. But it would have to be a serious enterprise, with decent times. For a very large number of marathon runners four hours is a symbolic number – a mark of achievement. The target times going through my mind were faster than that.

I floated the idea with mates and they all said: yep, we're in.

It was early December 2020. My Christmas deadline for Rob and his family to be secure was fast approaching.

The original plan was to run from Edinburgh, through Melrose (for Doddie Weir), and take a different marathon route each day, ending up in Saddleworth. But in those Covid times the messages from the local authorities were 'you can't do this, you can't do that'. If there were more than seven people involved it could become an event, and events were out.

My time at Leeds Rhinos had given me a good understanding of Covid protocols, so I copied them straight over to our challenge. If they were good enough for professional sport they would be more than adequate for what we were trying to do.

Phil Daly, who has been a huge part of the challenges, pulled the media and fund-raising side of it together. I planned five routes around Saddleworth and the other two in Leeds, as mapped out by Tom Hughes, a student at Leeds Beckett University. Among its delights was a massive hill after 19 miles.

It was thrown together. Forty-eight hours before it all began, we were obliged to go for Covid tests in Manchester. There were so many unknowns. We didn't have any navigation tools for the routes. We were just a few mates saying, 'Right, we'll have a go at this.'

It turned out to be a sensational experience.

Day 1 – we meet at the Farrars Arms, the pub in Saddleworth, at 6.30 a.m. The BBC were magnificent, really passionate in their support. They'd followed the story of Rob, Doddie and Stephen Darby right through. But the world had shut down and there was very little professional sport taking place. We couldn't advertise the routes in case the rules on gatherings were broken. At the BBC, Sally

Nugent, Dan Walker, Richard Frediani and Claire Ryan all grabbed it.

We ran the first four marathons around Saddleworth, Tuesday to Friday. Then went to Leeds for Saturday and Sunday, partly to avoid weekday traffic. We finished back in my home area on the Monday.

On day 1 we had three runners, two bikes and Phil. The six of us. That was it. A few people came out to clap us off but it was very low-key. Friends and family cheered us on our way.

We started day 1 on forty grand from a couple of sponsors – Rob's biggest backers from when he was playing. An item had gone out on the BBC that morning and I'd filmed a big interview in Oldham with Sally, all in the hope of letting Rob know how much we cared about him, and somehow getting us to the magic number for Christmas. By the end of day 1 we hit £100,000. Because we'd played around with the number 7 there were a lot of £7,000 donations. Goodwill was starting to sweep us along. Generally on these occasions sponsors get something in return for their support. All ours got was a name on a vest. When they made their commitments, they weren't to know it was going to be all over the BBC.

At that point there was no dividing line between the money that would go to Rob's family and the funds we would raise for the wider MND community. We were still in the early stages and all the money was for Rob. By the end of day 1 of the Seven in Seven we could see we were on to something special. We began to think about how things would pan out if money kept reaching us on this scale.

Because of the relationship we already had with the MND Association it made sense to think that everything we raised beyond Rob's needs would go there. We ran in the MND vest, so the connection was already obvious. Later, because of the new MND Centre that was being built in Leeds, the money would start going fifty-fifty to the Leeds Hospitals Charity and the association. We were given a big say on how the money was spent, from drug cure, trials, research and support for families who might need a chair-lift, wheelchair or new vehicle, to strengthening MND support centres all around the UK. The helpline was improved. We wanted something in there to support children and grandchildren, and money to go into memory boxes and voice boxes, which sometimes get overlooked but help ensure that people are remembered in the right way.

We were also keen to contribute to MND-SMART, a drug trial that ensured everyone with MND received some kind of new medication. In many trials, some were given the new drug and others the placebo. In this one, some people might have been given all five trial drugs, some people only one. But they could all be sure they'd be given real medication at some stage. People need hope, they need to feel they have a chance. If you're not sure whether you're getting a drug or a placebo you can't have that hope that the drug might just help you.

Throughout the seven marathons, every afternoon we had a Zoom conversation with someone with MND, through the association. I always knew we were running for Rob, but if I ever needed to be reminded of the wider aim of all those hours running across the hills of Lancashire in the rain, those Zoom calls drove the point home. The whole campaign became about the MND community. Those face-to-face conversations with families brought about the shift in thinking. They broadened our aims.

We'd finish the marathons around 11 a.m. I'd go home, jump on the watt bike, get in an ice bath, and then at 3 p.m. click on Zoom for an hour to talk to people with the illness, and their families. They weren't set up as a motivational tool for us. They were to help the families. But there could have been no sharper spur to get up the next morning and get going again, to help us see exactly why we were doing this.

Texts were coming in from Rob. And hundreds of other people. 'We support you. We saw you out today. It's wonderful what you're doing.' Hundreds of them. It was hard to keep on top of it all and reply.

Phil Daly has to take so much credit for pushing and driving behind the scenes. Throughout the trilogy he arranged so much publicity for us that at times I'd be thinking 'Hang on, Phil, I need to get my head together here', or 'I need the loo before I run.' Phil was a master at his job. I became used to him shoving a phone in front of me and saying, 'Can you just speak to so and so?'

And because the momentum built so fast I thought, by the end of the first marathon, there's a chance here that we'll be able to help not only Lindsey and the kids but other families too. I had no idea it would end up where it did. Some companies were on their backsides from Covid. Nevertheless the promises started piling up. And I knew we'd get to a million quid.

Rob could wake up on Christmas morning knowing I'd done what I said I was going to do. He'd know he could look after everybody.

After three marathons Jayne still thought the scale of the challenge was mad, but I was thinking, 'It's fine, I'll be able to do this' – as if three marathons suddenly equip you to run seven.

The night before day 4: I've hardly slept at all, tossing and turning, because my body is overheating – in December. Both the bedroom windows are wide open. It's freezing outside. Jayne is shivering in the bed. I'm on top of the covers in my boxer shorts with tubigrips on both legs, and I'm red hot.

Quickly I learned what running marathons for seven consecutive days does to your body. At bedtime I'd still be full of adrenalin and couldn't sleep. Apprehension may have been part of it. I'd done three marathons in three days in training but now I was heading into uncharted territory.

The torrid nights were a natural bodily response to multi-day endurance events. Apparently. Sally Nugent had put a call in to a specialist in the field and was given that explanation.

On day 3 I'd arrived at the start line at the Farrars angry, unshaven, feeling rough. I hadn't slept. I set off, quick. Way too quick. I knew how fast I needed to go to break four hours and was aiming to be close to 3hrs 50min pace to give us a buffer. But this time I ended up running most of it on my own. Chris Stephenson was running with us, but I'd left him behind. He was on his own. I knew he was all right because he had a bike with him and I had one with me. But still . . .

I have this memory of finishing and being upset with myself, thinking, 'It's not meant to be like this. I'm not meant to run angry.' I run quick when I'm angry or have something to fix in my mind. Back home, the feeling filled me: I messed up there.

Day 4, back at the Farrars, I pulled everyone together and said: 'I'm sorry, I messed up yesterday, I was out of order. We're a team, I got it wrong. I'm not making excuses. I'm knackered, I'm tired, I've not slept. But I'm sorry, I apologise. We stick together, we go together.'

Chris, who'd started me running, was among those in the huddle. David Spencer, who would also later do the whole Extra Mile challenge with me, had injured his calf before the Seven in Seven, so walked six instead, setting off at 4 a.m. every day. The final one he managed to run. My son Jack walked one of the legs with David, setting off with him at 4 a.m. Our two bikers were Darrel Rogers and Phil Allingan. A couple of guest riders joined us for a couple of days: Barrie McDermott and another old friend, Martin Wolstencroft. In Leeds, Jamie Jones ran day 6 with us. Jamie Peacock ran most of day 5. To have mates I'd been in the trenches with – especially in Leeds – was a godsend. When you have that kind of support your job's easy.

We started as a team, and it was important that we finished each leg as a team. Halfway through that fourth day, Chris developed a problem with his calf; but the fact that we'd had that conversation on the start line about sticking together changed the mood. It revived us. There was a really good vibe between us all. It could have gone the other way, with everyone cranky and resentful about my behaviour on day 3. Instead, we were back on song.

Not sleeping seemed to be part of the challenge, an aspect I simply needed to accept. With broken sleep you might get a couple of hours but you just don't feel right. That night, after day 4, I went to bed not worrying whether I slept or not. It wasn't going to stop me running. It wouldn't push my finishing time above four hours. And there was an interesting psychological twist. As soon as I resigned myself to the fact that I might not sleep, and that it wouldn't be a disaster, I slept peacefully.

All week Jayne and the boys were wonderful. Jayne was up at 5 a.m. with me for the two Leeds runs, slept in a room that was freezing, filled my ice baths, made sure my kit was washed and ready for the next day, prepared all my drinks, and sorted my food in the morning. It was clockwork.

The sacrifices the people around us make should always feature in the story of the running. So many other elements go into it.

Some indelible memories . . .

On day 5, we ran past the big fire station on Kirkstall Road in Leeds and all the firefighters were out to clap us on. Humbling.

At the end of that same day, Rob was there, as part of his BBC filming. His mural was up by then, and as we ran past it he was there in his chair, with Sally Nugent. He was there at the finish line too, which unleashed all my emotions. By now I'd run five marathons. That morning I had answered the alarm even earlier than usual to give us time to get over to Leeds. Seeing Rob and the family on the streets was overwhelming.

On day 6 we arrived in Leeds early. It was cold, dark, wet. Even darker and wetter than it had been in Saddleworth. It was the best run Jamie Jones could have done with me because I was struggling physically.

I've mentioned what a competitor Jamie Jones is. He'd never run a marathon before, but just said – I'm in. He ate a Mars Duo during the run. You know, the big one. I've never seen anyone eat a Mars Duo during a marathon.

There were moments during those days when I'd choke up, and not really know why. We all did. People might be singing as we passed, or a band might be playing. Suddenly I'd be overcome.

Once we'd completed day 6 I felt: we've got this, we can do it. Day 7 back home was going to be easy, fuelled by euphoria.

It was important to me to run through as many villages as possible in the area. To see a friendly face when you're in pain is such a help. On the Monday, the final day, back in Lancashire, supporters came across from Leeds to cheer. People beeped their horns, came out of their houses, clapped, cheered, shouted encouragement. It went from being something we'd knocked together and weren't sure we could complete to being this parade of human positivity.

In a video interview on the finish line I said: 'I can't thank people enough, because this is the cruellest of cruel diseases. And I know there are some wonderful charities out there, I know there are some horrible, horrible diseases and illnesses people have to face. But this is right up there with the worst. I've seen it close hand with Rob over the last eleven months. Our group, our team, our club, want to show how much we care about him. That's what this week's been about.'

The MND Association analysed the Seven in Seven coverage we received, the profile we finished up with. It was given a PR value of £23 million. The numbers were incredible. Much of that stemmed from the BBC. We were also on Sky Sports News, ITN, other sports channels and regional radio stations. We knew we had significantly raised public awareness for MND.

The glow stayed with me for months. For the first time in my life I could see how powerful it was for somebody's life to be changed that way when they needed it most, on the line between life and death. And very quickly I felt I wanted to do something else – selfishly, to some degree, because I knew how good it made me feel inside.

Doing things for other people is so powerful.

I understood that now.

And everything I'd done in my rugby career had helped to equip me with the physical strengths and psychological resolution to take on the seemingly impossible.

*   *   *

Many memories have stayed with me from that challenge. I remember we had been asking for updates all week on the fund-raising, how much money we were at. Phil would shout the figures through the car window, and it kept spurring me on. It made me feel: we've got to get this done, there are so many people behind us.

I'll never forget the moment when we were told we'd reached £500,000. That was huge. Christmas was sorted for Rob and his family. We'd amassed a surplus we hadn't yet thought about how we would distribute. Later, in April 2021, we'd learn that £2.2 million had been raised for the MND Association – way in excess of the £77,777 we had hoped to raise. The association would use £1.25 million for frontline services, £300,000 for local support in the north of England and £655,000 for research.

But there is one moment that's luminous in my mind.

On day 7, running round my home town, I was told we'd reached a million quid. And the news arrived just as we were about to run past my old school.

I looked up to see children thronged on the pavement outside.

Right at the front of them was my youngest son, Sam, smiling at me.

11

RUNNING WITH TIGERS

In my first week as a Leicester Tigers coach, I left home at 4 a.m. on the Monday, worked three days straight, stayed in the city on the Monday and Tuesday nights, then drove home on the Wednesday and said to Jayne: 'I'm not going back.'

I felt so exposed, thought I wasn't capable of doing the job, decided it was too much. And I have no problem admitting it, because it's a constructive message for others. I'd felt similarly vulnerable moving from Leeds Rhinos to Leeds Carnegie, and when starting at the Rugby Football League – being in a real job for the first time. Going back to Rhinos had been easier because I knew everyone there.

Feeling uncomfortable about joining the Tigers wasn't in itself a problem. I'd wanted to take a risk. But I just felt *too* uncomfortable. It was too much of a leap into the unknown. My only aim was to do a good job at Welford Road but now I had decided I would only let the club down, let the players down – and head coach Steve Borthwick down – by staying.

The following morning I called Steve, who was on his way to meet Eddie Jones, the England coach. I told him: 'I'm not coming back.' Steve acknowledged that I appeared to have made my mind up but still wanted to talk it through. He said he would call after his meeting with Eddie.

I liked watching rugby union but didn't fully understand it, which left me massively exposed. I'd sat in the coaches' meeting on the Monday and Tuesday mornings and didn't have a clue what they were on about. 'What is this?' I thought. They were talking players and tactics and systems. I felt disorientated.

On the Thursday morning Steve asked me to come back on Friday morning to discuss it face to face.

I said no.

He asked me to think about it.

But I could feel it shifting. Steve's way of dealing with it was beginning to have an influence on me. It was plain he really wanted me on his coaching staff. Jayne and my mum and dad were all supportive of the decision I'd taken, though Dad did say 'You've never quit anything', which rattled me, though it was said for the right reasons.

On the Friday morning, back I went, and agreed to give it a go. A couple of weeks later the squad set off for a training camp in Jersey. Steve and I went for a long walk on the beach and shared our thoughts. By now I was convinced I could give this a go. To get one thing straight, I was more than content being a number two in Steve's set-up. Particularly during Covid, there were things on Steve's desk I was more than happy not to have on my mind, because I'd been in that position. We discussed all that in Jersey. It was liberating not to have those responsibilities.

My policy was to admit to the lads when it was necessary: there are holes in my knowledge, some bits I'll get wrong. I framed it as a two-way street. I would be able to help them, but they'd also have to help me. I told them there might be moments when they'd want to laugh or shake their heads and ask – what is he on about?

They'd need to understand that my native tongue was rugby league.

Every time any union issue was discussed it might need translating. It was like learning a new language. In my head I was constantly going back and forth between the codes. I was still dreaming rugby league while these guys were dreaming rugby union.

The breakdown, when the ball carrier is tackled and other players fly in to join a ruck, was an esoteric new world I'd have to work to understand. And the scrum, which is a complex set of laws and techniques. Backfield play wasn't massively different. For a while I would look at the breakdown and not know what was going on. But equally that was true for some coaches who'd worked in union for thirty or forty years.

Steve understood from those first couple of days that he couldn't assume everything about my knowledge. Playing for Carnegie hadn't fully educated me in the ways of the fifteen-player game. But if you wanted to ask me how a tackle or a defensive system looked in league or union – I could tell you that. And I could talk plenty about attitude, how hard we'd have to work. I could give you all those bits. The intricacies would become clear to me with time.

The road to Leicester had started with another spell of feeling ill at ease. By Christmas 2020 I was enjoying the Leeds director of rugby job less. Cuts had been made and I felt I was constantly the bearer of bad news or forever saying no to people. I felt squeezed to the point where we were going to have to downgrade ourselves from a performance to a development programme.

There's nothing wrong with development programmes. They're vital. But to win in professional sport you have to have a performance programme. By Christmas I had decided I was going to do something else, after one more season at Rhinos, by which point I'd have done the three years I'd said I'd do.

There was no obvious next step. I didn't put feelers out. It crossed my mind to leave the game of rugby altogether. The one thing I knew I'd carry on doing was the MND fund-raising. I'd set my stall out on that. I would have been happy for that to define me.

During a morning walk near home in the spring of 2021

the phone rang. It was an agent I'd spoken to when I first retired. Did I have any interest in joining the Leicester Tigers coaching staff? I couldn't work out where the idea had come from, but replied, 'Yeah, I am.'

Two days later came another call, suggesting a meeting with Steve Borthwick. That went well. And in June it was announced that I'd be joining Leicester as defence coach.

I'd never harboured a burning urge to coach but had helped Shane Wilson and Darrel Rogers run Jack's local youth team. I was more drawn to that – watching the kids implement some of the things we'd taught them. I'd had a small taste of coaching the Leeds Rhinos first team as caretaker in 2018 in my time as director of rugby, but James Lowes was very much our coach on the grass.

So to then be offered a full-time specialist role in another sport was going to be a challenge. An accountant friend in Manchester has a saying on his wall by Richard Branson: 'If you get offered a job and you don't quite know what to do, just say yeah and work it out afterwards.' That's what I did. I thought: I can work this out as I go along. At least I had that understanding of defence from rugby league and had played seven months of rugby union. I was willing to graft, if the support was there.

All the coaching and support staff at Leicester were brilliant with me. Aled Walters, the head of performance, had won the 2019 World Cup with the Springboks, and was so willing to help and share. There couldn't have been a better environment to walk into. If they'd been protective, or seen me as a threat, it would have been so different, and very difficult.

Some will wonder whether they had me marked down as the next Shaun Edwards. Shaun is a Wigan legend who coached defence for Wales and France after leaving Wasps, where he worked from 2001 to 2011. He's been hugely successful in rugby union. I hadn't really encountered him on my travels but now it seemed a good idea to call him for background advice. We spoke for five minutes. My first impression: big Wigan accent, a jack in the box. I couldn't take in a lot of what he said. But I had a second chance to speak to him. This time he was relaxed and I absorbed every word. The second call wasn't a long one either, but he picked my brains too, on try-line defence in rugby league – something I would try to instil at Leicester (we conceded the fewest number of tries in the league in 2021–22).

Matt Egan, the head of performance analysis, is another on the Tigers staff I struck up a good relationship with. In the early days I'd whisper questions to him during Leicester games – 'What was that penalty for?' Brett Deacon, an assistant coach who works on our breakdown, was also a great ally.

When I accepted the job I reached out too to Phil Larder, another coach who had successfully worked in both rugby codes, and who used to teach at my old high school. I felt it was important to retain my faith in what I took across from league, to back my knowledge.

I might even say our defensive system at Leicester was modelled partly on Saddleworth Rangers under-15s in rugby league. Simple, stripped back. I kept being told how complicated people had made rugby union. But there are things in either code you simply have to do. You have to run hard, you have to hit hard, and you have to cover your mate's backside.

I kept telling myself: this is what we're going to do.

Across all sports, every defensive system has flaws that can be unpicked, but how hard you work for each other, and how you cover your mate's backside, is crucial. That's the bit I tried hardest to get across to the Leicester lads.

Mike Ford, father of George, was the defence coach I ended up replacing. I spoke to Mike as that was happening. He's from the same village as me. Strangely, though, I'd not had much to do with him, even though we were Saddleworth men who'd attended the same high school, albeit with an age gap.

My relationship with Richard Wigglesworth, the attack coach, and at the time scrum-half, couldn't have been better. There was no stronger attack–defence relationship in the Premiership. In fact, I'm going to say the world. We're both northerners, and we spent the nights when we stayed in Leicester talking, discussing rugby. With the friendships I've been able to build in the coaching room I've been so lucky. If they'd wanted to they could have set me up to fail. Instead they were so giving. The players too. I was in awe of how hard they wanted to work. That ethos was in place before I arrived.

I'd been at Leicester about eight or ten weeks when the media manager, Sam Williamson, who ended up coming on the Extra Mile challenge, said they could do with me sitting down for a media interview – more to discuss MND and Rob than the job at Welford Road.

The first question was: 'Do you believe good things happen to good people? Why has Rob got MND?'

Straight between the eyes. I couldn't answer it. It rattled me, and I was rarely off guard in interviews. I know how to answer it now, but I didn't then, in the heat of that moment. All I could say was that I'd need to come back to a question so profound.

Today, I would say there are always exceptions to the rule. I still believe good things happen to people who try to do the right thing. However, life sometimes throws things at people who don't deserve it; it seems to be part of human existence. I'd love it to be sunshine and roses, but when has it ever been like that? Even a look at people's lives in sport would tell you no one follows a perfect line. The norm is peaks and troughs, though the troughs are seldom as big as they have been for Rob.

My own next challenge was helping Leicester Tigers climb the table. Steve would probably say that getting the team from eleventh in 2020 to sixth in 2021 was a bigger process than moving them up from sixth to first. It helped that in that 2021–22 season we had an exceptionally good crop of young players to work with. Two weeks into my time there I came out of training saying four of them would all play international rugby that season. I was right on three of the four counts. I could see it straight away.

A rugby player is a rugby player. But if they have that spark in their eye – if they have an edge – they'll display the urge to bite down and show you what they've got. The mindset is clear, cold: 'I'm going to do this.' We were fortunate to have a lot of young players with that steeliness; and some experienced guys who'd tasted life at the top.

Put the two together and you have a powerful mix.

That 2021–22 season, my first, produced an impressive array of results. We began the campaign with an unbeaten fifteen-game run in the Premiership, Champions Cup and Premiership Cup. We won twenty of our twenty-four league games and conceded only fifty-two tries – eight fewer than the next best team, Saracens.

In the play-off semi-finals we beat Northampton to earn a place at Twickenham against Saracens, who had Alex Goode, Elliot Daly, Owen Farrell, the Vunipola brothers, Maro Itoje, Jamie George and Max Malins. They were formidable. George Ford, the season's leading points scorer, left the field after twenty-three minutes to be replaced by Freddie Burns, and it was Freddie's last-minute drop goal that earned us our first Premiership title for almost a decade.

It was odd, in the afterglow of that win, to think I might have left the club after just three days and not come back.

That final took me back to a place I thought I'd left. I never thought I would feel that way again about rugby – just so fulfilled and content. We'd come up against a brilliant team and we'd lost George Ford after twenty or so minutes, yet still prevailed. There was a level of adversity the team had come through. It took me back to that pattern I've talked about of fighting through turmoil at Leeds Rhinos.

After the game I went and sat on the team coach on my own. That weekend Jack was due to play on the Saturday. We'd made the decision that Jayne should go and watch Jack rather than join me at Twickenham. Then Jack's game was cancelled, on the Friday – too late for us to turn it round. But there was a family day at Leicester on the Sunday, so we elected to come together for that instead.

At Twickenham, everyone had filed over to the other side of the ground to a function room. Again, I just sat on my own, to have the moment. I called Jayne, called my mum and dad, then a couple of close friends who knew how tough the first two weeks had been for me. I thanked them all for their support.

I was so glad I'd stayed, stuck with it. There might be lessons there for people in other walks of life. Gradually a part of me emerged that thought not in league but in rugby union terms.

This is how I rationalise it now . . .

My attributes weren't great as a player, but commitment, determination and perseverance were in my make-up. And I can say with certainty that the challenges we took on for Rob helped my coaching. With the evidence of how the Rhinos lads came back together for Rob, I could stand in front of the Leicester players and say: remember how this feels, you'll have memories and friendships for life from playing sport. I could tell them: this shared history will be with you when there's nobody else there, when life has turned against you.

That was the foundation of everything we did for Rob, and it underpins my coaching. If the coach is willing to take on those challenges, believes in the cause, and is willing to run whatever distance he has to run to fight a disease, why shouldn't they run hard for eighty minutes?

Steve understood that too. And deep down I think he knew the MND work helped me as a person and as a coach. The connection with Rob makes it so much easier when I'm asking players to look after one another. In September 2022, when I did three legs of the Ultra 7 in 7 in training, some of the Leicester lads were fascinated. 'How does it feel running sixty-one kilometres?' they would ask. All the interactions helped me connect with them and gave us a topic of conversation away from the rugby.

At the start of the 2022–23 rugby union season I couldn't be sure I'd be at Leicester for years and years. One day that autumn I left home at 4 a.m. to drive to Leicester to coach, returned home, then ran 61km for the challenge. I felt I was juggling on several fronts. I'd like to have seen Rob more and have more time at home with Jayne and the kids. There were friends I'd like to have spent more time with.

Moving to Leicester would have made it easier. But always paramount was what is best for our sons. Sam started his Year 10 GCSEs in September 2022 and Jack was playing for Leeds, following that dream while finishing his A-levels. We needed to stay in Saddleworth while the kids completed their education.

The final leg of the MND trilogy of challenges was looming and Leicester had a title to defend in a season in which Worcester Warriors and London Wasps collapsed in mid-autumn. A league that started out with thirteen teams was about to be reduced to eleven. Some of those eleven survivors might have been wobbling too.

But you'll know by now that a life in sport is a tale of the unexpected. By Christmas 2022 I was no longer a Leicester Tigers coach. I was heading further south – to Twickenham.

12

THE EXTRA MILE

Rewind to 2020. My first challenge, the Seven in Seven, might have been remembered as a one-hit wonder. We'd built support for the message and I'd enjoyed that feeling of being back in a team. The communal support wasn't in doubt. I went home glowing for weeks from the spirit it generated between us. The messages kept flowing: do you remember this, do you remember that?

At the seventh and final finish line in Saddleworth a crowd had gathered in the road, a human obstacle around 50 metres short of the full marathon distance. There was only one thing for it. We were going to have to run right through them. There was no way on earth we were going to run less than the full marathon distance on the final leg. I thought: I'm not cutting it short here.

We ended up flying through the cameramen and every-body. It probably looked a bit rude. I wanted to finish it, do it properly. I didn't want my watch to show 42.1km. It had to be 42.2.

Jayne was there at the finish, with other wives and partners, and my mum and dad. Believe it or not, the following morning I missed not running, not being in that routine. My Achilles was sore but I promise I'm not making it up when I say I had the thought: I could do it again today.

It was the camaraderie, having that structure, having a cause again, being with people who are special to me. That next day, I trained. Mystifying, I know. But I'm a better person when I've trained. I try to do some kind of significant exercise every day. I didn't actually go out running again after the seventh marathon but I did enough exercise to tick over.

Feeling better about yourself through exercise is a big and complex concept. Why would that need be there? First, I'd exercised every day pretty much my whole life, so there's an element of familiarity and routine that's comforting. And, whether it's endorphins or serotonin release, I certainly feel better after I've exercised compared to before I've run or trained. People may laugh, but part of it in the post-playing phase of my life is so I can eat what I want. Jayne will see the difference in me when I've trained or haven't trained. There are very few times when I look to delay exercise until later in the day. I'd rather get on with it early, start the day well. On the rare occasions I let myself say 'I'll do it later in the day', I feel weak, as if I've let my discipline slip.

When I was playing, it was only in my mid-twenties that I allowed myself a week off. But I would still come back and beat my fitness scores from my own personal training. I knew what got me fit. At the back end of my career, the rower did that job for me.

The oval ball game is stop-start. There are only short intervals in which to recover. I knew that with my fitness I could go effort after effort after effort. And I'd be able to go longer than anyone else. In my mind that was my super-strength. When the game changed and my role altered I knew I had the ability to feature in every play. The only one who could perhaps say the same was Jamie Jones, who was extremely fit and competitive. The benefit was being able to recover lightning fast after a spell of exertion in a game.

I was asked once about going to that dark place of pain and exhaustion. Not many people like going in there. But I like going in. It makes me feel good about myself.

If we go to a theme park or a water park as a family, I'll find the biggest ride, the biggest slide, and I'm on it. I have nothing to prove by it, but I'll look for the biggest test. If you tell me I need to go into the dark place, I'll go straight in. I won't delay it. All these different fears and worries: we build them up too much. You go in, and it's never as bad as you've told yourself it's going to be. The challenges were proof of this: as soon as I started one, the doubts, the desire to still be at home, disappeared.

143

The little man on the shoulder asked me from time to time: 'Why are you doing this? What are you doing this for? It's five a.m., shouldn't you still be in bed? Why are you on the rower again? Let it go.' But the exercise I do isn't to slay demons. The minute I don't want to overcome the urge not to bother, the urge just to walk away from exercise, I've lost what I'm about. Lost what fires me up, gives me my edge. Is it my stubbornness? I am definitely very disciplined in how I approach most things. The tougher the road I go down – and I found this in my playing career – the more fulfilment is waiting for me at the end. Those feelings have carried through from rugby into life and certainly into the series of challenges to help Rob and others with MND.

Without those characteristics, maybe I wouldn't have been able to push myself to the extremes that helped make life a bit better for Rob and his family. Maybe my personality type has its uses.

There is, of course, a selfish part to it. The campaign gave me a chance to be back in a collective. A chance to give hope to other people. Retirement turns you back into an individual. You retain the bonds of friendship but you lose your membership of a team.

MND is such a terrible illness, and destroys people so quickly, that I sometimes feel guilty about taking any personal fulfilment from the challenges. I've questioned that. Should I be deriving so much from it? Is that normal?

One thing I do know. We were never going to stop after the Seven in Seven. By the time the third challenge came round in November 2022 I was preoccupied with getting the MND Centre built for Rob, in Leeds. I wanted him to be able to open that building. At the same time I was eager to carry on helping people who've been diagnosed with MND. I wanted to put pressure on the government to release the £50 million they'd promised for research into a cure. I've also been attuned to the need to back off sometimes and pace our efforts, because I'm aware how many charitable causes there are. They all need their share.

Before we could think about challenge no. 3, though, we had no. 2 to deal with. A new quest, bigger in scale, and tougher. It was to run 101 miles in twenty-four hours, the one on the end being the 'Extra Mile'.

People have busy lives and work pressures. And the reason the Extra Mile was done in one day is less romantic than you might think. I'd started my new job that summer, at Leicester, and couldn't ask my new employer for a whole week off. Had I not just joined Leicester, with a serious role to play, we might have dreamt up a different adventure.

This is how it came about . . .

Jamie Jones had sent me a copy of the *Backyard Ultra* video, not to suggest we do it, but for my entertainment. As soon as I saw it I knew there was the germ of an idea in there. The Backyard Ultra is a marathon where the contestants have to run 4.167 miles in less than an hour. Not

once, but consecutively. And it carries on until the last runner or runners concede or fail to finish. Twenty-four laps
equate to 100 miles. The record when I started looking at it
was ninety laps. Later it passed 100. Some of the partici-
pants go for four days. It's just incredible.

The euphoria from the Seven in Seven made us all want
to go again. We just didn't know how, or where. It was on
my shoulders to come up with a plan and lead it.

'What's next?' they all kept saying.

'Leave it with me,' I'd reply.

When I started ringing round mates and suggesting we
run 101 miles, they asked, 'How long are we going to take
to do that?'

'A day,' I said.

Incredulity. 'We're not going to be able to do that, are we?'

'Why not? Course we are. Course we are. We'll do it.'

To get a team together for this one was a challenge I
wasn't sure I could meet. Injury loomed as a serious threat.
An Achilles, a calf – those are the crucial bits you have no
control over. But in my head it wasn't complicated: there
was nothing that was going to stop me running 101 miles
in twenty-four hours. In my body, maybe, but not in my
head.

Nobody said, 'Yeah, that's a good idea.' But a few thought
it might be a bit of fun after another tough year for everyone. As the days went on we continued to do calls with
families who had been affected by MND. That was tough.

It was inspiring but also painful seeing what these families were going through. It made it so much more important to come up with a new plan and see it through.

Covid put an extra wave behind us, pushing us on. People wanted relief from the darkness; they wanted to reconnect, fight back, see a future.

My obligations at Leicester needed to be taken into account. I wanted to finish the season as director of rugby at Leeds Rhinos. That meant a lot to me. But that would mean starting at Leicester in early November, two months into their season. Leicester was un unknown world to me. I didn't really know anyone there. Joining in November might be too late for me to implement anything or have any influence. We also had a half-term holiday booked in October. Jayne was adamant we needed a family break – and she was right. But I needed to hear it from her to make it happen. It was probably going to be our last family holiday with Jack, who had just turned seventeen and was about to start his pre-season with Leeds.

I was juggling.

So I spoke to Steve Borthwick and Leicester, who were massively accommodating. The solution was me sitting down with Leeds and giving them detailed plans for the next few months to allow me to leave early. That enabled me to join Leicester on 1 August 2021. Steve said they would honour my holiday. They'd moved some goalposts for me.

I didn't feel I could then ask to step away from Leicester for another week in November, right in the middle of the campaign. Hence, I needed a twenty-four-hour challenge, a spectacular to grip the public again after the Seven in Seven. People needed to feel it was enough of a challenge for the fund-raising effort to be evolving into new and exciting forms. Each time we were having to raise the bar.

I wondered: can I break 100 miles down into hourly 7km sections, once again as a nod to Rob's shirt number? Within twenty-four hours I could then hit the 160km mark. That's it. That's what I'm going to do.

There were no Covid restrictions. We could run wherever we wanted. Jayne wondered how far it was from Leicester to Leeds, between the two rugby clubs. I'd already thought of running from Leicester to my house – 106 miles. Jayne reiterated the value of running between two clubs that meant so much to me. I typed it into Google Maps. It was around 100 miles. A crazy coincidence.

We had our plan. Run the 7km sections every hour on the hour. We'll be all right, I said. I felt like Mike Bassett, the fictional England manager in the film, using the back of a fag packet. There was no science behind it at that stage. It was a great idea, but could I do it?

No idea. The furthest I'd ever run was the marathon distance. Now I was jumping from 26 miles to 100. It was enough of a test to excite people.

The support staff began to form. And when Tom Hughes at Leeds Beckett planned the route it came out as 101 miles. That's where we got the title of the Extra Mile challenge from. It landed in our laps.

A lot of my work at Leicester as defence coach was about running, and how you defend when in tough spots together by covering each other's arses. I couldn't frame the challenge that way to Steve when I asked for 22 and 23 November off, but I didn't need to. He couldn't have been more supportive.

'What do you need?' Steve asked.

He got it. He understood it. He saw how important the team was to me, my old team at Rhinos, the players I'd played alongside. In the coaches' office at Leicester nearly all of them joined for at least part of the 101 miles. The club was right behind it. We already had Doddie on side and now Leicester's support helped bring rugby union right into the picture alongside league.

BBC Breakfast again grabbed hold of the idea, and my phone started to flood with messages. That was when I began to understand the difference we were making not only to Rob but to the MND community as a whole, and to people who'd had a rubbish year.

As the planning developed we worked out that I was going to run each 7km section in anywhere between thirty-five and fifty minutes. We didn't budget for some of the legs being a bit shorter and some being longer: it was important

149

to accommodate suitable rest points. The longest was close to 9km. Trying to run that in an hour when you're fifteen or sixteen hours in is a real stretch, especially when you can only rest for three or four minutes. That one changed the whole dynamic of the challenge.

Phil Daly came up with the idea that at each of the stops, a bell would ring two minutes before you rose from your chair or left your tent to go again. They used that in 'Mad Dogs' marathons. When the bell rings, you make the start line, and get it done.

At each location someone with an MND connection would ring the bell. We had sufferers, carers and family members who'd lost somebody. That was a step on from the Zoom calls in the Seven in Seven. The bell ringers turned out to be a vital element of the Extra Mile.

You couldn't ignore that call. Hearing that bell, I could never think: I don't want to get up and run any more. Some of the stories about people using the bell in the Mad Dogs told how they associated it with good things in their lives: a treat from the fridge, or a cuddle from their wife. They'd trained themselves to make a positive association with something that was actually sending them out for another shedload of pain.

The bell, an old school bell, was provided by the Leeds Hospitals Charity. After it was over they presented it to me encased. And that gave me the idea to place it in the MND Centre in Leeds when it was built. I knew it couldn't yet be rung to announce that a cure had been found, but it could ring out for special occasions and achievements and become a powerful symbol.

It could be rung by so many people up and down the country connected to this illness – this cause.

13

THE APEX OF PAIN

It was the hill, a huge hill out of Nottingham, that told me: everything had changed. The realisation hit me head on: this isn't a fun run any more, we're in it now.

Physically, trouble had shown its face far too soon into the challenge. Mentally, I knew I was about to go somewhere new, to a place that would stretch the resolve I felt so sure I'd built up over the years. You think you can handle anything, but you're not always in control of what comes round the corner.

As soon as we began to climb out of Nottingham, I could feel my calves start to rebel. Stage seven of twenty-four legs. Number seven – Rob's number. The magic number we had built this whole challenge around. The instructions had sounded so easy, so routine:

7. Leave Nottingham and head towards Mansfield. Along Cheapside before turning up Clumber Street, Milton Street

and Mansfield Road. Follow the A60 until we reach Carrington then turn left on to Hucknall Road (A611). Carry on along A611 past Nottingham Hospital. Leg ends at Bulwell golf course.

In the training run we did – twelve hours – I hadn't once felt rumbling in my calves. Now I could feel panic rising. As we climbed out of the city it just seemed to be hill after hill after hill.

By stage seven we'd already run a marathon. The pain in my legs was starting to grip. My thoughts were: shit, I've bitten a bit more off than I can chew here. Did I get my training wrong? Without anyone seeing it in me, anxiety was taking hold.

On the pain scale it was perhaps two or three out of ten. But I knew a two or three out of ten by stage seven was going to turn nasty pretty quickly. I didn't have a great deal of injuries in my rugby career – a couple of calf tears and a few broken bones. And after the Seven in Seven all I had was a sore Achilles for a fortnight. I knew that if my Achilles went wrong now on top of the calf trouble this journey would be murder to complete.

I was baffled. Two weeks before on the twelve-hour training run I'd run a lot quicker than this. We had with us a nutritionist from British cycling, James Moran, and in everything we talked about there was no mention of electrolyte use. We felt we'd get enough from the carb intake.

But some instinct made me put electrolytes in my bag just in case. At the point I reached out for them we'd just come up this massive hill and jumped in the mobile home to get my calves freed up by the physio, Dave O'Sullivan. It was like Popeye reaching for the spinach. Mentally, more than anything, I needed those electrolytes.

Halfway through the next stage, I felt them working. Relief flooded through me. But it must have been psychological. Any expert would tell you electrolytes shouldn't kick in that quickly.

At the same time I changed my trainers. That helped too. I went back to my brighter pair – fluorescent yellow. I always think, if you're going to put a pair of trainers on to run, they've got to make you smile, feel good about yourself. The brighter the better.

Ben Jones, the great sports scientist we were working with, kept saying – we're running too quick. I knew what pace I wanted to run and we were going a lot slower than I wanted to. If we ever ran 101 miles in twenty-four hours again I'd run a lot quicker. The new people and those who ran with me kept getting a bollocking for going too quick, but it wasn't them, it was me, because I was at the front of the pack.

It sounds crazy when you've got twenty-four legs to do to say 'I want to go quicker.' But your body is used to running at a certain pace. There was a balance all the time between running quicker and getting more rest, or running slower and getting less of a break between stages.

As with the Seven in Seven, the mantra I had in my mind all the way through was: make the start line, just make the next start line. I knew that if I could get out of my chair every time that bell rang, and greet those people who were there to share in that moment – people from the MND community – I'd finish the leg.

The hardest thing was getting out of that chair. Most people say the hardest thing is turning up. Most people have days when they don't want to go to the gym, or don't want to run hard.

I'd prepared myself for that test, though. All the way through the 101 I drew on the lessons of my playing career. There was no way I was going to surrender. Just no way. I was representing Rob. Didn't want to let him down. Didn't want to let the team down. Didn't want to let my family down. The BBC were behind it. The MND community were there. The funds were ticking over, the awareness was growing.

I just couldn't fail. It wasn't an option.

I knew I was carrying all these responsibilities. And I knew by stage seven that it was going to get hard.

I'd said I wanted it to be horrible. And I really meant that. I wanted to show there are people who are willing to go through pain for some greater good.

'The Apex of Pain' was an expression I picked up in the summer of 2021. I've always believed in physical sacrifice as the basis for success in team sports. The phrase features heavily in a documentary about the marathon runner Eliud Kipchoge called *The Last Milestone*. There's a section in that documentary that makes a point coaches need to impress on players: in their physical commitment, they have to go that bit further than the opposition are willing to.

When we put the Extra Mile together I knew it needed to be extreme, to make that point about pain and commitment. It couldn't just be an exhibition run. I was asking people to give. So I needed them to see how much I was willing to give of myself.

Did I prepare properly? No. I'd run only once above marathon distance in my life – the twelve-hour training run, or half of the Extra Mile challenge, in the form of twelve 7km runs. Looking back, that was crazy. Yet somehow it added drama to the story. I hadn't had nine months to prepare for this. There was no clearing of the diary. It wasn't a carefully mapped-out expedition. It was a leap into the dark.

The big message was for Rob, and for all those in the MND community. They didn't ask for what they had. Those who have died from MND had no say in what happened to them. The families who looked after them weren't given a choice. This was a chance for me to show them that there are people out there willing to put themselves through it so others with fatal diseases aren't fighting alone.

I wanted Rob to know I was willing to do anything for him. I met so many people in the MND community whose stories and pain were horrific. I wanted them to smile in my discomfort. I wanted it to give them a glow inside that our team were willing to go through hell too.

I was suffering because they were suffering.

Somehow, after stage seven, we felt a resurgence. There were a couple more hours of daylight left. I can remember the turning point, in this big group of people running and talking, with music blaring. At the bottom of a big hill, everyone left us. There were three runners, plus two on bikes. Martin Wolstencroft, who had the stereo, needed to charge it, so we lost him for a while. We ran up the side of a dual carriageway, single file, into a headwind, cars streaking past, unable to see much, thinking: we're in it now. All the time I carried the thought: if I fail, where do we go from here? We couldn't allow it to end.

The night before, when we gathered in the Holiday Inn in Leicester, we'd had a bit of a briefing. I spoke to the team and said, 'At some stage tomorrow someone's going to get angry. They'll say something they don't mean, but it's because they're tired.' What I meant was – *I'm* going to get angry, *I'm* going to say something to someone I don't mean. Please don't take it personally.

Someone was bound to get cranky. As with most blokes, when you mix tiredness with being hungry it's a volatile combination.

I was aware there were some who hadn't been in a rugby or football environment and wouldn't be familiar with the banter you get in those settings. The fact that stick's coming at you means you're part of it – you're accepted. As long as it doesn't cross a line, of course.

As far as I'm aware, Tom Hughes, who planned the route and accompanied us on a bike, hadn't been in that world before. He was a triathlete – an individual sport. He was perhaps not used to that kind of exchange. I did warn him at the outset: every time we hit a hill, people will come at you, but they don't mean it the way it sounds. It's banter. If you get us lost, everybody's going to come at you, but they don't mean it. It's just comedy.

Most of the stages we wanted to be 7km were bang on. And we wanted good safe places to stop. I had requested that there shouldn't be a big deviation from 7km, either too long or too short. Jayne came out to meet us at 9 p.m. in South Yorkshire. We'd just done an 8.5km slog. I really needed the toilet. I jumped on the loo and had only three minutes before we needed to get going again. I had tears in my eyes, thinking: Jayne's driven all the way out with my dad and I've not got any time with her. I apologised to her and said, 'Next stop, I'll have longer with you.'

We hit the road again, and the next stage was 8.5km again. Once more Jayne had driven ahead to meet me.

I wasn't happy – and said so.

Tom didn't take it well.

I was mumbling to myself.

'Tom, my wife's come out, and we've done two eight and

a half Ks. I asked you not to do this and we've done two on the bounce.'

By now it's maybe half eleven at night.

Tom went from being at the front, all bouncy, on his bike, to riding at the back. Darrel Rogers, my good mate, came up and rode next to me. He knows me well.

'Tom's a bit upset back there,' he said.

'He should be 'n' all,' I said. 'But send him up.'

Tom pedalled up to the front of the pack. I apologised. I told him, 'You knew this was coming. I told you last night. Now pull yourself together, we need you, you need to lead us.' Within minutes he was bouncing again alongside us.

Many visual images from that challenge stayed with me. At half past midnight we lost our way and had to take a detour through a graveyard. I'd never run through a graveyard in the early hours of the morning.

People were out at two and three and four in the morning, in dressing gowns, banging pots and pans the way they did to support NHS workers during Covid. We passed through old mining villages that might have lost their economic purpose. But the people in them hadn't lost their kindness. Gemma Phillips, our doctor, told me people were pushing money through the windows of our cars, which turned into mobile bank deposit boxes. Our staff were counting the banknotes and rolling them into wads. They used snoods and anything else they could find to make bags to store the cash. The generosity was astonishing.

What went on at those times surprised me. People were hanging out of windows shouting. People were playing music really loud at 3 a.m. In one village we ran past a parked police car with our music blaring. The officers slid out of the vehicle and wished us all the best. There was no 'Can you turn your music down please?'

We ran into a Tesco car park in Clowne where the motorhome was and were surrounded. A brass band played.

There were people taking pictures through the windows. Sore from cycling, Darrel needed to put some cream on his bits. Down went his shorts. He started rubbing. Outside, people were taking photographs through the windscreen of him in action.

Our convoy of vehicles became so long that we would have to cut it back for the Ultra 7 in 7. At one point during the Extra Mile it was so long that it showed up on satnav as a red line of traffic congestion – in the dead hours of the morning.

There were lots of different rugby league shirts. Maybe eight clubs. All brilliant. A man in a Salford jersey started running alongside us on the opposite side of the road. We called him over to run with us and he was soon in the swing of it. Three miles down the road he must have realised 'I've come too far', turned and headed home. I hadn't known there were so many Leeds fans in South Yorkshire.

Music was indispensable. Songs were played over and over. We had 'Suspicious Minds', 'Billie Jean', 'Come On Eileen'. The cyclists were all older than me, so at times it was very Smooth FM. Plenty of Elvis. When he joined us, Alastair Campbell asked for Dire Straits. We had Bee Gees, and then . . . 'Your Song'.

I'd met Prince Harry several times when he was patron of the Rugby Football League in my time working there. I was the one charged with looking after him and explaining certain elements of how the sport was run. I got on great with him. At his wedding, to which I was fortunate to be invited, Elton John had played at the reception. That night on the run, 'Your Song' came up on one of our playlists. It became a bit of an anthem.

On the endless road, special people kept emerging from the gloom. Gareth Ellis and Keith Senior, team-mates and good pals I hadn't seen for maybe eighteen months. There were people who came out who were team-mates of Rob's and mine. Each one inspired me. They'd all done their own charity work. Keith has run plenty of marathons, Gazza has done bike rides. Jamie Peacock came, Jamie Jones, Barrie McDermott. When Rob was diagnosed it pulled everybody back in. You retire, disperse, go on to different chapters in your lives, and yet I always knew the core group would be there when I needed them. And that they'd need me too. In true friendships you can go a long time without seeing people, or even speaking, but you just know they'll be there.

Some of them were turning up at two in the morning, some at four. I knew they were there for Rob. I knew they were there as well for me. They didn't get much back from me in terms of chat. I was pretty cooked. But just to have them alongside me gave me the strength to go on.

Once you got sleepy tired, I was warned, everything would seem 40 per cent worse. I had to keep reminding myself of that advice. The toughest moments were with seven hours to go.

Seven, again.

It was dark, it was cold, my quads had pretty much given up. In my mind I did the maths: I've got 50K still to run. Just over a marathon.

How can you run a marathon when your legs aren't working? That's when I knew I was in a battle. The challenge was, I'd never been in a war like that before. I'd been tired and fatigued but never with seven more hours of effort to go. Yes, with thirty seconds left on a rowing machine, or a couple of minutes still on the clock in a game. But never seven hours.

At that time of night it feels like for ever.

That's the autopilot switch. There were people I wanted to talk to, people I wanted to thank, people who'd come out to support us for those last hours. Physically I couldn't do it. Couldn't communicate.

I was just trying to survive.

I'd expected this level of exhaustion. And I got what I

deserved. I didn't want to let those around me down. They were looking to me, looking at me, probably questioning whether I could get through.

Yes, there was doubt in their eyes. They'd probably never admit it to me. Even my wife, my brother, Darrel on the bike, would have felt a creeping uncertainty. But another part of them knew that if I had to crawl to that finishing line, I'd crawl to that finishing line.

In my playing career, the medals were brilliant, the Grand Final rings great. But they're in my mum and dad's house. The things that mean most to me are the memories and the friendships. I know I can go years without seeing someone, but when we meet there's that glint in their eye. There's something there. It's not that typical friendship. Sport – being part of a team – gives you something deeper.

Again, it's to do with adversity and coming through ordeals together.

I had far more adversity than success, than good times, but I wouldn't change that fact. It's to do with my make-up. On some level I wish it hadn't been that way. But you are what you are. You get over disappointment by thinking: I'll show people. I'll show myself.

What was adversity to me? Something that causes pain, that's unpleasant.

Poor performances.

Injury.

Being dropped, or left out of squads.

Things that cause embarrassment or shame.

Most of the top sportspeople around the world will have something that tripped them up, and which they had to fight their way through. You understand it and learn from it. Sometimes you just get smacked in the face. Everyone gets their turn.

On the shoulders of our Leeds team settled a constant burden. It certainly settled on mine. I perhaps carried that burden too much. You need to be accountable and you need to take responsibility for things.

Sport is a brilliant career but it can be brutal. In what other walk of life are you judged by thousands of people every week? Most players find living with that, dealing with it, understanding it, accepting it and thriving off it, a daily challenge – not one that's often talked about while the games are coming thick and fast.

In a rugby league shirt, I knew what to draw on. I knew what to say to myself. I knew at certain times I was going to cop it.

As night turned to day again, heading into Leeds, I was conscious of welling up, on live TV. I suppose you want people to look at you and see a strong guy? Is that a fault some men have? In the Seven in Seven, at certain moments I was crying as I ran – but there were no cameras, nobody with us. It was all right to let loose and nobody would know. For those last couple of stages in the Extra Mile there were lights, cameras on us, a lot more people around. In Leeds, because the streets were full, I didn't want people to see too much of my discomfort.

You spend your playing career telling yourself lies about how tired you are. Lies expressed through body language. In both codes of rugby, the minute you show fatigue you get targeted. So you spend a lot of time trying to pretend you're not tired and you're not hurt. If you betray 'weakness' it comes at you even more.

Over those last seven hours I dreamt of finishing, imagined the last stage, with just one more run to do. We came out of Wakefield, at Belle Isle, and the former rugby league great Garry Schofield appeared. Garry got a chant going. By that stage it all felt surreal. We were perhaps an hour from finishing, I'm exhausted, it's six in the morning, there's 150 people there, and Garry Schofield is leading a chant.

There was another guy called Gary, from Rochdale. He had a different strain of MND. Gary had taken a taxi from Littleborough to Leeds because he wanted to ring the bell at the start of a stage. I can remember him gripping me just before we set off and giving me a big cuddle.

He wouldn't let me go.

This guy, who I'd never met but had seen on TV, and who'd been diagnosed with MND, came all that way in a taxi at half past four in the morning to be there for six o'clock. And he was incredibly moved just by being there.

I knew we weren't far away now. Everybody was beeping their horns.

The plan for the final stage sounded gentle, routine. It wasn't.

24. Leave Hyde Park and travel along Headingley Lane / Otley Road (A660) before turning left at the War Memorial at the Original Oak / Skyrack corner. Turn left down St Michaels Lane towards Headingley Stadium and entering the stadium via Gate E, South Stand and entering the pitch via the South West corner.

I'd never felt like this before. I knew I'd taken my body somewhere it didn't like. And taken it there for a long time, not just a couple of hours.

On autopilot you keep telling yourself: just one foot in front of the other, keep going forward. I was happy we weren't far away. Touching distance. It's starting to get light again. The people you see are a bit more familiar. The places are more recognisable.

Leeds isn't the city I'm from. It's not where I live. But it looked after me, shaped me, supported me. To be able to finish there and run through parts of it that meant so much to me was special. In all that pain I felt swept along.

I was in agony. So tired. In the BBC documentary *Kevin Sinfield: Going the Extra Mile* shown in early 2023, my physio, Dave O'Sullivan, admitted that he thought I'd been in serious danger of collapsing. I felt drunk, but I had enough 'lights' still on and could start to feel the glow inside that we were nearing the end. I still wasn't sure how we'd got to where we now were. But we weren't far away.

Most people could see the pain in me as we ran towards Headingley. Anyone could see the emotion. I spent my whole time during that final stage fighting back tears, welling up and holding back, welling up and holding back, because we had got it done. There was a bigger message in my stubbornness. My body had had enough. If I'd needed to keep going, though, I'd have done so till I dropped.

Rob was in the stadium. I'd known he might be there at the finish but hadn't had it confirmed. I was attuned to how much his condition could fluctuate. I knew that Macy, Rob's daughter, would be there to run the final part. I'd love to have been able to speak to everyone in the throng but I was just hanging on. Macy was brilliant, she wanted to run. There wasn't much left in us. She probably doesn't realise how enjoyable she made it for us – this young girl, full of life and energy, with this big smile, who represented everything about her dad, so proud to be there, to be part of it.

For a young girl she has an incredible awareness. The minute we came into the stadium, Macy stepped back. She wanted to give me the moment. But to me it was about all of us. I beckoned her to stay next to me. I wanted her to be with us, and for her dad to see us, Lindsey too. I was trying to get them all with me.

Individual awards are fine but it's the team stuff that has always mattered. My name was all over this run, but without the team I wouldn't have made it to the end. Many had spent their own money to be part of it. They didn't have to do what they did. Many of them went through similar hardships to me.

I know for sure that if I said to each and every one of them 'We're doing it again this weekend', they'd be there.

My boys Sam and Jack were in the stadium, along with Jayne. Jack was in the stands with the Leeds Rhinos squad. Jayne and Sam held the finishing tape. My mum and dad and brother Ian, who ran the last couple of legs, were also with me.

All my feelings crystallised. I wanted Rob to keep fighting and I wanted to inspire him, just as he's inspired so many people. I wanted him to still see what our friendship meant.

He's seen me tired. Lots of times. He's seen me in difficult moments. It was important that he saw me the way I was at the end of those 101 miles. I thought it might help him to see that a part of me probably was broken, but my spirit was, like his, ready to fight.

There were parts of him that didn't work as well as they should. But his spirit was absolutely there.

I stepped across to him by the finishing line, lowered my head to his. At first I tried to have a bit of a joke with him because I knew he would be emotional. I told him the seventh leg was the most difficult and that it was all his fault. I didn't tell him how tough it was. I told him how glad I was to see him.

At any moment I was ready to burst into tears.

Since he'd lost his voice we had shared many text messages. It was easy to communicate. Face to face, it was difficult. We had found a different language to keep us connected.

As players, we never made long speeches.

It's a look.

Eye contact is enough.

You truly know someone's ready from the look you get from them. That eye contact is so powerful.

I'd look at them before every Grand Final and they'd look at me. You knew you were in it together. You scrap and you do what's necessary together to get the job done. Sometimes you're not good enough. But the fact that you're willing to go there is what matters.

When it was over, I staggered away from Headingley and changed out of my kit back home in the garage. I'd been sweating for over twenty-four hours. The garage has always been the place where the two boys, when they're caked in mud from football or rugby, would get changed. Everything goes in the washing machine in the garage.

I found myself completely naked, and I can remember Jayne pushing me upstairs, shoving my backside up step by step. I thought: this is where we've ended up. I'm getting pushed up the stairs.

Jayne put me in the shower. In bed at eleven in the morning, adrenalin still racing through me. I was in the place I had wanted to be for so long. Finally I slept. For two hours.

The best way I can describe my phone is that it was like after winning a Grand Final: 400 text and WhatsApp messages, tons and tons of emails. I was mind-blown trying to respond, trying to take it all in.

My body was battered, shot, but in many ways that was the feeling I had missed from playing. You'd play on a Friday night and get very little sleep because of the adrenalin. You'd open your eyes at six, satisfied if you'd played well, or won the game.

It was the moment I always felt free. Free from it. Free from any pressures or stresses. There aren't many times when I've had that in my life, that contentment. And it doesn't stick around for long. But that morning in bed at home I was just content.

Then I started thinking about what we had achieved. What we had set out to do was crazy. It's amazing what the mind will do if it really, really has to.

And we had to. There was no 'Oh, sorry, we've miscalculated this, we've got it wrong, we'd better turn back.'

We were in.

If we'd failed, I'd have gone again the week after, until I'd done it. I wouldn't have let people down. I'd have let people see me fight and scrap to get it done.

I can live with not winning. Sometimes people are better than you. I can live with not being quite good enough. That goes back to my childhood. I wasn't the best at anything,

but I knew I could make myself more committed than anyone else.

But if I'd failed that day, I'd have gone back out and done
it again. Or kept going back until I'd finished the job. I'd
have just carried on.

I knew this wasn't the end. Even before I walked into
Headingley I knew there was going to be more. The week
before we did the Extra Mile I visited Rob. His dad Geoff
told me: you've done enough. It was lovely for him to say it,
but that could never be.

Was it enough? It's never been a crusade. It was always
about showing someone I cared about them, showing them
respect. I felt a sense of responsibility too to the MND community. So many kind people came out of nowhere to
engage with me. The letters I get, the emails. People hunted
my email address down, goodness knows how. 'We're having this event in, say, Ipswich . . . can you come to it?'

There will come a time when I can't run any more, when
I will struggle, but my mind will always compete. I've never
been someone who wanted to compete with others. I've
always competed with myself. That's the bit that's driven
me my whole career.

So when Rob's dad said to me 'You've done enough', I
knew what he was saying. He was genuinely worried about
what we were taking on. But I know as well that he understood what was driving me. What he was saying to me

wasn't as profound as the feeling a father would have for a son, but it came from deep friendship.

There'll come a time when I can no longer take on the physical challenges, when the hills of Nottingham would defeat me. But for now, I knew we could always find new ways of helping. Long runs wouldn't be the only option. We'd just need to keep using our imagination.

14

JAYNE, JACK AND SAM

My son Jack, who made his senior Leeds Rhinos debut in April 2022 at the age of seventeen, was born three weeks before we won the 2004 Grand Final and was at Old Trafford for that victory. His only knowledge of it will be the picture I have of him, Jayne and me in the stand celebrating.

To think of a three-week-old baby falling in love with rugby league would be pushing it, yet Jack was to follow my path into the Rhinos starting team at a similarly tender age. His first full senior appearance was at Castleford Tigers on Easter Monday, nine months after joining Leeds from Saddleworth Rangers just down the road from us. He wore the same no. 32 shirt I wore for my debut, when I was sixteen, and the interim head coach was my old mate Jamie Jones.

The symmetry stood out on that special day for Jack and us. The road to it stretched right back into his early childhood. Our other son, Sam, didn't aim for a life in professional sport but is no less special for that. Jayne and I have been blessed with them both.

If I said Jack saw 300 of my games at club and international level, that would be a conservative estimate. From the age of two he went everywhere to watch me. The minute he knew what his dad's life was about – the wonderful game I was part of – he wanted a rugby ball all the time. He loved playing football too, but most of all he wanted to be at the games I played in.

When he was six, a year younger than I was when I first tasted the game, I took him to Waterhead, my boyhood club. But training there changed to a Friday night, which clashed with a lot of my Leeds Rhinos games. It wasn't fair on the other kids for Jack to miss training on Friday because he was watching me play, and then be picked for the Waterhead team that Sunday. I know what other parents are like. It wouldn't be fair on Jack either to open him up to a barracking. Plus, he needed to train, to learn and improve.

So Jack had to move clubs, and I was desperately sad, because Waterhead is where I was from, where I played all my junior years. We brought him to Saddleworth, close to the streets where we lived. That helped. It was a new path for him. Although he was still 'Kevin's son', there was no affiliation between me and Saddleworth Rangers. He could claim that new space as his own.

Jack played at Saddleworth from then until October 2021, when he joined Leeds. We'll always have the fondest memories of the people who looked after him at Rangers. Sadly the coach, and a good friend, Shane Wilson, passed away in 2021 from cancer. It was a big hit for that age group, a trauma for them to work through. Shane, or 'Jocky' as he was known, was a huge influence. Lovely guy. He understood Jack's situation in relation to my status in the game and knew how to handle him at some of the away games where comments might be made.

Darrel, who was another of Jack's coaches, was to become a huge support to me on the first two challenges, joining me on a bike. His son played in the Saddleworth team as well. For two years the three of us coached them together. I was more the water and kicking-tee carrier but that didn't diminish my enjoyment of being with such fine people. Working with those kids and seeing them get better was what turned my mind to coaching when I retired.

Jayne and I were quite young when we started a family but that suited us and fitted in with how I wanted to live and dedicate myself to the job. The big nights out? I didn't really have any. Maybe one a year. The temptation therefore was to start a family early. Our thinking was that when we reached our forties we'd have more chance to catch up with things we wanted to do. Not so much reliving our twenties as embracing things that were relevant to that stage of life.

It worked for us. For Jack to be so immersed in the rugby life and gripped by the game was a bonus we had no reason to expect. Game day was his favourite day of the week. He couldn't wait for it. He went in full kit, with Grandma and Grandad most of the time, especially when Sam was born and Jayne stayed at home with him.

Jack would watch the game intently. In the stands, he wouldn't have a handheld device to distract him. He knew what was going on from a very early age. He studied the game. The minute I walked into the players' bar he'd be drenched in sweat because he'd been running round for an hour with other kids with a rugby ball in his hands.

Driving home at night he'd be asleep in the back in his full kit. I'd climb in the back of the car to lift him out, risking cramp, and carry him in and put him to bed. Then the following morning he'd be a chatterbox about the game the day before.

By the time he was four or five, during school holidays, I'd occasionally take him in for the last team session. You've never seen a kid so excited. He was more excited for the team run than he was for Christmas morning. He'd take his own little ball and kicking-tee. After training, when I would stay to practise kicks, he'd be out there with me, on the Headingley pitch, kicking goals. He couldn't get enough of it. It's probably fair to say he loved it more than I did.

Sam, when he talks about it now, sometimes wishes he'd paid more interest to rugby. That's not a regret on my part. He still remembers plenty. The boys were different in that respect. Sam was never really into rugby, or at least never fancied playing. He'd wear the kits, but in a different way, and I quite liked that. Jack would perhaps look at him and wonder, 'What's up with you, why don't you fancy a bit of this?' But I loved the fact that Sam wanted to play with his trains or his cars. When I came home I had a lovely mix of one who wanted to play football or rugby in the yard and one who was happy with his trains, though Sam did also join us for those games out back.

At Leeds games on a Friday night especially, Sam loved the singing, loved the chanting. Coming into the bar and seeing them both in their kits, picking them both up, was the perfect way to end the evening. I treasure the photographs of them with the trophies we won. After our second Grand Final win in 2007, Jayne was a couple of months away from giving birth to Sam, so I had a Grand Final ring for both our sons.

Jack's a lot like me in his personality, the way he goes about things, and Sam is just so laid back. The contrast is pleasing, good for me, good for us as a family. Sam's equally unique and special.

The common denominator, of course, is Jayne. I couldn't have hoped for a better wife, companion or friend. We met when I was twenty on a night out in Oldham. Within nine months we were living together. We became engaged at Niagara Falls on a trip to see my aunt and uncle in Toronto. She thought I was joking when I went down on one knee and told me to get back up.

Without her I couldn't have done any of it. She sacrificed everything for me and the kids. The boys know it too. The fact that Jayne has been willing to forgo a career so I could make the best of myself in sport, while making sure the kids had everything they needed emotionally, has been her gift to us all.

The more time Jayne and I spend together, the better we are as a couple. Some couples might say the opposite is true. But with us, the more we're in each other's company the better we get on.

When Jack signed for Leeds in 2021, I was constantly emotional, wanting to burst into tears. It may have been an age thing. Anything to do with him and the game would cause me to well up.

When Jack made his Leeds debut, we'd trained at Leicester that day and I'd left early to get there in time. It happened so quickly I didn't have time to churn it through. All I wanted was for him to do all right. I wasn't worried about him physically. I knew what he was capable of. The coaches at Saddleworth had done an expert job. I knew exactly where Jack stood on the scale of challenges.

Covid cost him most of his under-16 year, when he trained with me a lot, in the garage. We did two Zooms a week of real hard slog with his Saddleworth team. We got stuck into them. It was hard for me, but Jack was flying, so I knew he was in a good place physically, fit and strong.

But he'd never played against men before and you don't

know how they'll manage when they do. When I made my debut at sixteen the game was more physical than it is now. You have to be super fit to play now. Back then you needed to be fit too but there was an even bigger requirement to be big and strong. The dark arts were still flourishing. People were still getting away with bits and bobs.

At sixteen, I wasn't ready. I may not have been ready at eighteen either. But I needed to have a taste of it to see what it was about.

If I look at rugby league's potential development over the next ten years, I'd actually prefer Jack to have made his debut in the era when I came on the scene. Because of the number of players playing contact sport, across all sports, and the concerns about concussion, I'm not sure about rugby's longevity. For a young player the question then becomes: do you want to spend the best part of your twenties chasing a dream that could collapse at any moment? Or should you be taking a different path?

I've stood on the touchline since Jack was seven and heard people scream things at him because he's my son. I see it still, at reserve and academy level. There are people taking pot shots at him – because of me. They're trying to score cheap points, but unfortunately it comes with the territory.

I never succumbed to the temptation to stride over and confront anyone who was goading my son. With the role I had, it was always in my mind that I was being watched, that my behaviour was being scrutinised. It showed the kids how people should respond in those circumstances. Everyone wants to hit out and fight. That's an instinct. But I seem to have been put together with a degree of patience and tolerance, which makes it easier to turn the other cheek.

I've seen the same spiteful behaviour towards other people's sons. I think that's where we are in society. Over the past four or five years in both codes there are more players who are ex-professionals' sons. All of those young guys get treated differently by spectators and sometimes people in the game. Jack understands that completely. He wears the knowledge that people are going to go after him. He's always handled it. He always *will* handle it. He's grown up with it and manages it brilliantly.

Nevertheless it was a concern for me when he moved on to Leeds. It helped that I had left the director of rugby role there by the time Jack signed for the club. It allowed him to plough his own furrow. All along I've said to him: you'll either be good enough or you won't. It's that simple. But he's talented enough. He has a really good way about him. His head's screwed on.

He juggled the way I did with education and professional sport. But it's been more difficult for him. He was in with the first team two or three days a week. The flexibility his college gave him during Covid meant he could do his academic work at night. On a Saturday evening he would put four hours in. In his first year of A-levels he got excellent grades off the back of 50 per cent attendance in college. For us as parents, seeing him work so hard was moving.

It's my job and Jayne's job as parents to make better versions of ourselves. That doesn't mean to say 'better rugby player than I was'. I absolutely feel as a parent that I want to help make our sons better people than I am. I want them to pursue their dreams and do what makes them happy. The fact that Jack is on a path in rugby now is brilliant and I'll support him, give him everything he needs, if he wants it. If not, I'm just his dad. The same with Sam, in whatever he wants to do.

My message to them both is identical. Just do your best.

15

BACK IN THE RACE: ROB ON THE STREETS OF LEEDS

The idea of racing Rob through the streets of Leeds in the summer of 2022 in the world's most high-tech wheelchair surfaced after the 101-mile challenge.

The CEO of Leeds Rugby Foundation (the charitable arm of Leeds rugby), Bob Bowman, got in contact to say there had been a request from Run For All, Jane Tomlinson's charity: would you run the Leeds 10K, then the Yorkshire Marathon in 2023? Jane, who was born in Wakefield, was acclaimed around the world for taking on endurance events while she was in the grip of incurable cancer. Her last great challenge was a 4,200-mile bike ride across America in 2006. She died at forty-three after raising £1.85 million for charity

'Absolutely,' I said.

Lockdown had brought about a noticeable dip in Rob. Throughout the pandemic I was conscious that he wasn't on the vulnerable list. He should have been. But people with MND weren't included. That worried me. I didn't want to be the person to take Covid round to his house. As soon as the world opened up again, and I could get to see him more regularly, the first couple of minutes were tough. It was a shock to see how little he could walk, function, or even drink.

As Covid receded, more of our old pattern returned. By June 2022, before the Leeds 10K, I was seeing a lot more of him. One Friday before Leicester played Newcastle on the Saturday we went together to the site where the new MND Centre was going to be built in Rob's name. On that visit I studied Rob intently to gauge his condition. I always give him a cuddle, or touch his shoulder, because it gives me a sense of his weight.

For the previous six months there had been no bulletin to say he'd gone dramatically downwards, physically. Lindsey said he was 45 kilos; in his playing days he had been 70. When I arrived he was wearing a T-shirt. And he never wears T-shirts. And everything was . . . skin and bone.

Rob looked like a very old person who was fighting hard to keep going. But his massive beaming smile told a more encouraging tale. I thought: how can you smile, with this body that's giving up? He wasn't able to move anything. When I went to his hands they were clenched into claws. His feet didn't move. His mind, however, was unaffected.

I mention the physical details of Rob's illness because it's important to face and understand what MND is. Take, for example, the twitching, the fasciculation. Everything is rippling. The muscle fibres in the neck, everywhere. It's as if there are spiders underneath the skin, constantly moving. To see it is . . . crazy.

When Rob's breathing, it sometimes sounds like he's laughing.

Nobody wants to see a friend who's thirty-nine, with three children, in that condition. Each visit I make stays with me long after it's over. I think about him a lot – and constantly on the journeys to and from work. And when I read his texts I can almost kid myself it's not real, because he talks so normally in messages. His thoughts are the same as ten years ago. But I know we are in a very different place.

When I ask Rob a question I have to condition myself to be comfortable with uncomfortable silences. Fortunately I've never worried about trying to fill a void with noise, or speak for the sake of it. When you're there with him, it can take him an age to reply, unlike with the text messages, which are instant.

A lot of the time I already know what he's thinking. I mentioned earlier about people from Yorkshire saying exactly what they think. Well, Rob was at the stage where he would say precisely what he thought, without preamble. Often it would make me laugh. And sometimes it made me cringe. I'd be thinking: you can't say that.

I'd even say it to him: 'You can't say that.'

The reply would fly straight back: 'I can say what I want.' But it would always be laced with humour.

When I leave him, I'm uplifted. And I'm sad. A whole range of emotions runs through me. It gives you a massive dose of perspective for your own life, when you see the challenges he has and what he's doing to keep going, how he's fighting. It's really easy to come away from there thinking: yeah, my crap doesn't matter.

Often I wouldn't see the children because Rob would be at his mum and dad's. Lindsey goes to work and takes the kids to school, then Rob to his parents' house. They would do a lot of the talking for him, and he would sit there laughing or winking or rolling his eyes.

In the early stages I would be constantly looking for signs: what can I see that shows he's getting worse? People were always asking me: 'How is he?' I wanted to give feedback but I didn't want to tell them everything or provide a running commentary.

Small bits of involvement in normal life would give him a boost. Awards evenings, though, would sometimes stretch his enthusiasm for getting out and about. Even as a player he was never a fan of them. In 2022 there was a 2012 reunion dinner which also honoured the 1972 championship-winning Leeds team. I texted Rob and said: 'If you're going I'll drive back from Leicester and take you.' Joking, he said: 'I'd have to go with my dad, and my dad can't feed me that well, so it ends up down my front.' Pretty matter of fact.

However hard the communication is, the connection is

unbreakable. I'd swap texts with him every couple of days. He was fully aware of what Jack was doing, completely up to speed with the Leicester news and results. He still watched lots of rugby and asked me questions about Leeds Rhinos. He was still across all of that. He would send me daft jokes. He'd give me blunt answers to questions about how he was. Honest, and blunt.

Three sites were being considered for the MND Centre in his name. One stood out. You could feel it as soon as you went up the drive. You'd want to be proud of putting an MND Centre together, proud of going there, not ashamed. Don't put it at the back of a hospital, round a corner. It should be front and centre.

Seeing where the centre would go meant a great deal to Rob. He sent me a startling number of texts on the subject. An example: 'Why are we all continuing to fight? You don't know the difference it makes. It keeps me fighting.' This was stuff I wouldn't expect him to say. Stuff I wouldn't expect him to feel, because he had so much going on physically. But the fact that he kept texting me to say how important what we were doing was for him – for him to keep fighting – helped sustain me too.

When we first talked about buying a special chair for Rob, the Yorkshire Marathon was foremost in our minds. Tom from Leeds Beckett University, who helped me on the Extra Mile, said he would investigate suitable chairs that could provide us with a comfortable chariot. The best ones were made in France, but because of Brexit and Covid there were endless complications getting one over to us.

After I ran the Manchester Marathon in April, I had trouble with my knees and kept it quiet that Rob and I were going to do the Leeds 10K. If the chair didn't turn up the pair of us were going to look ridiculous. There would be no way of getting him round. I was also thinking – my knees are a mess here, but if the chair turns up I'll run it.

I had a chance to run in Greece on holiday in July, which gave me the confidence to think that if the chair turned up, we were in business – we'd do it. It arrived at Rob's house on the Thursday night before the race.

A cross between a lightweight wheelchair and a Paralympic racing vehicle, it's an ingenious creation. It allows Rob to be fully strapped in. We had it designed in blue and amber, the Leeds colours.

When I turned up and lifted Rob into the wheelchair we were going to run with, the knowledge struck me deeply that Lindsey was having to do that every day. I, on the other hand, might have done it once or twice. It brought home the condition he was now in. That's why I ran as we did in the 10K: quickish, desperately, perhaps with fury about what was happening to my friend.

They sat him in it and said: 'He's comfortable.'

'Right, we're going,' we said. No trial run.

Sunday morning: 'Right, get in the chair, this is how the brakes work. Away you go.'

The fifteenth Leeds 10K started on the Parkinson steps at the University of Leeds and finished at Leeds Town Hall. In all, 110 Leeds Rhinos fans, support staff, ex-players and volunteers were raising funds for the Rob Burrow Centre for Motor Neurone Disease. Just over 4,000 people took part. My time pushing Rob was faster than my first Leeds 10K time just after I'd retired in 2016. We did it in just over forty-four minutes.

For the start we were ushered to the front of the grid past a line where all the runners were lined up. They clapped us in. The MC gave us a special introduction. People along the route were all behind us. Other runners on the route, as we passed them, or they passed us, were so inspired by what Rob was doing.

He'd been wanting for a while to get involved in events but a normal wheelchair just isn't conducive to going at any speed above walking pace, let alone going over speed bumps or potholes. It went as well as it possibly could have, though it would have given him a sore backside from going over the bumps. There was no shortage of fun along the way. I got the impression from him that he liked being around fit, athletic people. The smile on his face from the pictures was one of pure enjoyment, and it stayed there the whole way round.

The next day he sent me a text. 'I loved it pal. Hope you felt OK with it. You are superhuman pal and you are the best of friends. I'm up for a marathon if you are.'

I replied: 'Of course we can do the marathon together. I'd be honoured.'

I could tell, he'd had an uplifting day.

For him to have a challenge to focus on was hugely beneficial. And he knew I would push him every step of the way. It helps us both. In the dressing room, Rob was a mixture of very private yet mischievous and cheeky. Funny. A chatterbox. Yet underneath he was always quite a solitary character.

Rob's messages often bring a tear to my eye. He will convey huge gratitude. He can't understand why people are being so kind to him. Never once has he said to me: why me? Never once has he shown any sort of anger or resentment that MND picked him out. I find that remarkable.

It has given me a chance to reflect on every aspect of life and find perspective in the highs and lows. Seeing him, and being confronted with the visual evidence of his disease, removed that false sense that life was continuing for him with at least some degree of normality.

I've never shied away from the difficulty of witnessing that deterioration. It's human nature sometimes for people to find reasons not to visit, to avoid the profound upset you feel when you leave. But I couldn't contemplate not seeing Rob, no matter how bad it gets. He needs to see me there, and probably needs to see all of us there, as he did that Sunday on the streets of Leeds – the community, with their applause and their support.

It helped when Rob acquired an Eye Gaze, a screen with a camera that picks up the user's eye movements as instructions. Those eye movements activate letters, words or images. The Eye Gaze allows Rob to send texts and WhatsApp messages, change the TV channel and say things out loud which come through in Rob Burrow's automated voice. Doddie Weir started using one a few months after Rob.

Rob could now communicate, but it wasn't conversation. If I asked him a question, by the time I got the answer the conversation might have moved on three times. You get a sentence back, then trace it to an earlier part of the conversation.

Before we could plan our next joint outing we knew we'd need a pit stop. There were adaptations to the chair we would need to make. The heels on the platform for his feet didn't quite keep them in position. His sunglasses kept dropping down his nose, so we would need elastic ties. And if we were going to do a marathon we would have to find a way of feeding him and giving him drinks. And communicating.

Here we were, then, thinking excitedly about running a marathon together in May 2023. I wasn't blind to the stats: a third of MND sufferers die in the first twelve months; 50 per cent die within two years. By now we were two and a half years into Rob's illness. If we reached May 2023 that would be three and a half years.

But by putting goals in front of him – landmarks might be a better word – we gave him incentives to keep going. He was fully aware of how powerful the effects his appearances were having on other sufferers.

Now he had the chair I hoped he'd join us for the next leg of the trilogy, even for a couple of kilometres at the end of a leg. It didn't have to be a massive appearance. He could cross a start or finish line.

Rob's garage was already full of chairs, so the luxury one, from France, which cost six grand, was kept at Leeds Beckett University. There, it would open up avenues for others to take part in sporting events. The chair – the Rob Burrow Chair – would be the means of transport. It would acquire a wider use in the community. It would carry someone with a serious disability into an event, a race, a better day. They would no longer be a spectator at something they couldn't take part in.

In that Leeds 10K, Rob wasn't just an observer stationed in a wheelchair as hundreds of other people flowed past, having fun. He had his bib on. He was a participant. And at the end he collected his medal like everyone else. One of the great Leeds Rhinos players was doing what he'd always done in his sporting life. He was back out there competing.

16

MY DESERT ISLAND

'Sir Kev' was a label pinned to me by Leeds fans, who'd seen me in their jersey from when I was thirteen. I wasn't from Leeds but sometimes would be seen as more 'Leeds' than the Leeds lads. The supporters viewed me as one of their own. It was humbling, and at times a bit embarrassing, to be known as 'Sir Kev', even if it was laced with Yorkshire wit.

It sounds trite to say external recognition isn't something you go looking for. But when it comes, you wouldn't be human if you didn't feel proud to have made a mark outside your chosen sport.

An MBE came first, in 2014, news of which arrived after we'd been out as a family to Alton Towers. At home there was a letter that, judging by its stamp mark, was obviously important. Whatever it was, it wasn't going to be a letter from the Queen. A lot of people said they thought it was from HMRC and I probably assumed the same. A tax letter in a white envelope rather than the usual brown.

Jayne ran a bath for the kids while I started going through the post . . .

Rugby had given me countless special moments without me needing to seek them outside the game. An MBE felt like a nice embellishment to my playing career. I didn't grasp the meaning of it until the day we went to the palace: me, Jayne and my mum and dad.

To receive it for services to a sport I loved to bits felt a bit bizarre; especially in a team sport, where individual awards can't possibly count as much as the trophies the team have won. But I felt massively humbled. At the ceremony I was separated off with people who'd given fifty years of service in important fields. I'd played just nineteen years of rugby, yet found myself in the same room as all these wonderful people who'd given masses back to society. Later the OBE was, I believed, very much for the Seven in Seven, for pulling it together during Covid and exceeding expectations in terms of awareness and fund-raising. It was for the Seven in Seven team – for all of us. And this MBE was very much about the Leeds Rhinos team that had won so many trophies in that period.

Mum and Dad are republicans. Buckingham Palace wouldn't have been their natural political home. Yet they too had a lovely day when we all went to collect my MBE, which surprised me. They understood what it represented, where it came from and what it meant for the club and the team. They knew it had a wider meaning than the purely political one of whether we should have a monarchy or not.

They couldn't come for the OBE because Covid restricted participation to one guest per recipient. It was Jayne's birthday. Rob's fund-raising game had been on her fortieth and she'd willingly postponed the celebration in favour of the match. For her forty-second we found ourselves at Windsor Castle rather than Buckingham Palace. For both investitures Prince William was the giver. Second time round, it was more intimate, and special. This time I was able to stay with Jayne in a room of about twenty people, all of us masked.

Everyone wanted to talk about Rob.

They'd hoped to honour us together, but Rob couldn't make that date.

For the MBE, I don't think Prince William knew who I was. I didn't expect him to. For the OBE, he knew about the runs. After the Extra Mile, Harry sent me a very nice email about how hard he'd tried to pull league and union together – and was delighted to see we'd been able to do it. That was something I was particularly proud of. (For the Ultra 7 in 7 we'd be trying to pull not two but three codes together: football, through Stephen Darby's involvement, as well as the two forms of rugby.)

* * *

My second place in the 2015 BBC Sports Personality of the Year award is often thrown in when I'm introduced at an event, and I always make a joke of it. I used to say, 'Andy Murray is meant to be the bloke with no personality. Try coming runner-up to him.' (Having met him, Andy is of course a really nice chap and fun to be with.) Finishing second in the BBC poll was a great experience; and it was beneficial for the sport to have the first rugby league player nominated.

We had a brilliant night out after the BBC ceremony. I'd been playing rugby union for Leeds Carnegie for three weeks when I took a flight to Belfast for the show. All the Leeds Rhinos lads came. I'd been gone from Headingley for nearly two months.

After a Grand Final, the lads tended to go wild. You get the bus back to Leeds and away you go. But as captain I always felt I was still on duty. Someone needs to keep their wits about them. At the function, somebody's got to be able to stand up and talk some sense. Plus, my kids would be there. So, after a Grand Final I'd always gone home after the function with Jayne and the kids. The following day there would be a homecoming. Then I would go out and have a few drinks with the lads.

On the Monday morning after my final game – the 2015 Grand Final – we were flying early to Dubai for a break, then I was hoping to go straight to Carnegie and rugby union. So, on the Sunday, I left the next-day get-together after four or five drinks, saying goodbye to friends who'd been drinking for thirty hours straight. Some were a bit teary to see several of us leave the club. When people start crying on your shoulder it's probably a good time to go. But after that 2015 Grand Final win I had this nagging sense that I hadn't had a chance to spend enough time with the great team I would never play with again.

Belfast and the BBC ceremony rectified that. The lads' flight from Leeds-Bradford had been delayed for three hours so they all got on the ale. They rocked up at this hotel in Belfast smashed. I knew they were all due to go up on stage with me and was worried there might be an . . . incident. Thankfully they were very well behaved.

Later they drank the BBC's post-show party dry. But they were magnificent. There was an 18ft Christmas tree and I remember that coming down. That was our lot. All in good jest. I love those lads, and the night was so important to me.

SPOTY is staged just before Christmas, and because I was flying from London to Belfast straight after our away game at London Scottish, we decided that I would go on my own. I remember seeing Tyson Fury up close, and talking to James Nesbitt and Martin O'Neill, who said he loved his rugby – people you'd never normally meet. The Christmas tree still gets mentioned when that night's brought up.

* * *

In October 2022 I made an appearance that grew in importance to me when I started to understand whose footsteps I was following. For me to be on *Desert Island Discs* was partly down to it being a Rugby League World Cup year. My dad was so excited. He wanted to pick my tracks. 'No, this is me going on, not you,' I had to tell him. When you look at the people who've been on the show over its eighty-year history you see what a big deal it is. The research call alone lasted three hours, covering my early life, my career and the forthcoming Ultra 7 in 7 challenge.

It felt surreal. What humbled me was being told I was the first rugby league player to appear. And then being asked to sign the guest book, which has been going since 1942. As I added my own name I looked through some of the others and saw Bono, Adele, Tony Adams, Kate Moss. On the train home I went online for the full list of people who've been on. That was a pleasing way to spend a journey.

On one level it's massively awkward to be a castaway because your music taste is quite personal. I wasn't bothered whether people liked my selections but to come up with eight songs that had a story to wrap round them was challenging. You couldn't just say 'I really like this one'. All the while you're conscious of coming across in the right way.

The presenter, Lauren Laverne, asked me about rugby league's 'tough guy reputation' contrasting with 'the thread of friendship – and love'. I talked about players needing to trust and rely on one another. I kicked it off musically with

'Jerusalem', because I first heard it as a schoolboy in 1992 at the Challenge Cup final.

For 'Come On Eileen' I may have surprised a few people by describing myself as 'a crazy five- or six-year-old charging around the lounge in my little white vest and boxing gloves while Dexys Midnight Runners played in the background'. Van Morrison's 'Someone Like You' recalled the music my dad and I would listen to on the countless journeys from 'deepest, darkest Oldham', as I called it, to Leeds for evening training.

These are the tracks I chose . . .

1. 'Jerusalem' – a big rugby league song
2. 'Come On Eileen' – Dexys Midnight Runners
3. 'Someone Like You' – Van Morrison
4. '7 Days' – Craig David
5. 'I Think We're Alone Now' – Tiffany (because it's Jayne's favourite)
6. 'Baker Street' – Undercover
7. 'Last Request' – Paolo Nutini
8. 'Fix You' – Coldplay

To keep me going on the island I said I'd need a couple of chickens a day. 'You'd be lucky,' Lauren said. The luxury item I chose in the end was a self-propelled treadmill. Hardly a luxury, Lauren pointed out. 'Last Request' was the track I said I'd save from the waves if I had to, because it reminded me of so many good times and being back in a team for the first two MND challenges.

And the book, which I've mentioned before in these pages: *The Edge*, by Howard E. Ferguson, with quotes from 750 of the world's most successful competitors. Dean Bell called it his bible. Inside the front cover of the copy he gave me he wrote:

To Kevin.

I hope this book helps you in your career like it did mine. There is so much to learn in rugby and in life – my advice to you is, always be honest with yourself. Hard work makes dreams come true.

In difficult times, religious people turn to the Bible, the Qur'an or whatever sacred text is central to their beliefs. I would turn to *The Edge*. I'd read a couple of bits and feel better about myself or the situation I was in. The man in the mirror was an important concept, later in my career. Being honest with yourself.

The fact that Dean gave it to me added to its value. He was a great player, an inspirational one, who had captained a fine Wigan team. For Dean to get the Leeds job was fortunate for me. He saw some bits in me that made him want to give me the book. He also gave me my debut as a sixteen-year-old and the following year coached me in the academy. Just a great man.

My time on *Desert Island Discs* ended with a brief conversation about a subject I didn't want to get into in that setting. But I accept it's an issue that won't go away. Head injuries, concussion – the ever-present worry many rugby players will carry into later life.

17

THE HEART AND THE HEAD

The reason I was reluctant to talk about brain injuries on *Desert Island Discs* is that I try to be careful about drawing connections between contact sports and damage to the head. It's not something I like to offer up to headlines when so much research is still being done.

I'm someone who's been knocked out a number of times and I'm conscious of some of the challenges that may confront me and others down the track. But I wouldn't change any of that, wouldn't swap my life in rugby. Perhaps a professional player could say with some justification, 'I didn't know what I was signing up for at the time.' But I don't think you can then use that retrospectively in potentially the wrong way.

So, on Radio 4, I didn't want to respond to such a big question in a compressed space of time. I didn't want to run the risk of suggesting we understand the subject inside out and can address it in ninety seconds.

How the sport might look in five or ten years is something I'm conscious of every single day. Whatever role I've had in rugby I've tried to think first and foremost about what it's like to be a player – always to put myself in their boots. On the training pitch and in games I know what we're asking them to do. My thoughts always revolve around balancing risk.

I talk regularly to players in my care about the fact that player safety has to be integral to what we do. There are drills we have to go through in training to get them ready to play, but we try to perform them safely. If I ever thought we weren't doing it with safety uppermost then it would be time for me to move away from rugby coaching altogether.

We have a duty to look after those coming after us and make the game we pass on to future generations as safe as possible. Right through the coaching set-up at Leicester the club was aware of players' lives. I won't say players' welfare, because it's much deeper than that. I'll say players' lives, because lives are at stake. They may not be now, in the game being played in front of you, but in ten or twenty years' time the ramifications might creep up on people.

The attitude to repetitive contact has changed massively in recent years. At Leicester we were well below the maximum level of physical impacts allowed in the protocols. We could get enough good stuff done without having to 'go live' (replicate match intensity) every single day. I don't believe in doing that on the training field. I never have. In rugby league when I was a player it wasn't something I believed was necessary to bring you to a peak for a game.

Training sessions where people smash into each other relentlessly are history. The bulk of the defence work we do is with the tackle shield, very rarely body on body. Even then we never do more than four-minute blocks. I believe in quality over quantity: a couple of good, technical tackles, then move on.

In the past I was part of rugby league sessions where you were knocking the stuffing out of each other. But that changed significantly in league and now rugby union is following the same path.

I'm fully aware of the litigation being pursued by ex-players in rugby league. I played just short of 600 games and am cognisant of how many bangs on the head I'd have received in that time. Twice I was knocked out cold. I can still remember waking up from those blows. I'm aware of what could befall me later in life. But equally I'm not inclined to retrospectively challenge a sport when I'm not sure the sport itself knew the risks or consequences. The medical science – or evidence – wasn't necessarily there.

We've always known how precious the brain is, and that injuries can be serious, but it's only in the last few years that the awareness has reached a level where structural change is made urgent by the science. We need more work on it.

There are some potential benefits to the spectacle itself. If collisions and bulk become less of a factor in the game then players might become a bit lighter and quicker. The Rob Burrow type of player might come back into fashion. Those who can no longer fall back on physicality may need a new super skill to secure their place in the sport.

At the RFL I was in on a number of calls with and swapped emails with Professor Willie Stewart of Glasgow University, who'd been doing work on brain injuries in Scottish rugby union. Willie's a great guy who convened a seminar for rugby league players through our past players' association. I sat in on it because I helped put it together. We had twenty players join us on Zoom. Only twenty players from the last fifty years. And none of the seventy taking legal action were on that call. Some might not have known it was on, or possibly were out of reach. But we have to help one another as well as ourselves.

The encouraging part of Willie's work was his message that you can do things to mitigate risk. He listed ten environmental factors, such as regular exercise, a balanced lifestyle and good sleep patterns, to either offset the dangers or change the path completely. He put a lot of minds at rest – mine included.

One of his reassurances was that just because you lose your keys, or forget somebody's name, it doesn't mean you have dementia. It can just mean you're getting older and your mind and body aren't working as well as they did. Reductions in mental sharpness are issues not only for rugby players but people in all walks of life in middle age.

It's a shame more people didn't hear his talk.

Yes, all leagues and contact sports could probably do more, but in the last couple of years both league and union have substantially increased their welfare provision. They've had to. The lesson from injury and litigation in the NFL in America suggested it was bound to land on rugby's governing bodies too. The more evidence we have, the more informed decisions will be.

A concern for me is that we might change rugby beyond recognition or close an avenue that gives boys and girls a chance to play a team sport with incredible values. There are unintended consequences with most activities in life. But if we shut rugby down we close down the environment and the culture I grew up in, and which gave me such great friendships and memories. And if we stop rugby as a recognisable contact sport we'll only create another societal beast in some shape or form.

18

THE SEVEN ULTRAS

It was the day of Rob's fortieth birthday, 26 September 2022, when we announced the biggest and toughest of our running challenges.

BBC Breakfast broadcast the news, with Sally Nugent interviewing Rob, Doddie, Ed Slater and me. 'Welcome to the dream team,' Rob said to Ed, who still looked undiminished by the disease but was already squaring up to its implications. Physically, Ed admitted to Sally, 'there are small signs of the things to come'. He went on to confide that 'The impact it has on the family is difficult.' Doddie also reinforced the point about the effect it had on loved ones.

The news was this: starting on Sunday 13 November we would run over 60km per day for seven days from Murrayfield Stadium in Edinburgh to Old Trafford in Manchester in an Ultra 7 in 7 challenge. Inspired by Rob, Doddie, Stephen, Ed and all those living with MND, we would have an initial aim to raise £777,777. The press release laid it out:

The Ultra 7 in 7 challenge will support five charities which support people affected by MND, and invest in research to bring us closer to effective treatments and a cure for the disease. The main beneficiaries will be the MND Association and Leeds Hospitals Charity's appeal to build the Rob Burrow Centre for MND in Leeds. However, there will also be donations to MND Scotland, My Name'5 Doddie Foundation and the Darby Rimmer MND Foundation plus support for the 4Ed campaign to support former Gloucester and Leicester Rugby Union player Ed Slater, who was recently diagnosed with MND.

The whole challenge will build to an incredible finish as Sinfield enters the field at Old Trafford at half-time in the Men's Rugby League World Cup Final on Saturday 19 November to complete his challenge, having visited Melrose, Newcastle, Middlesbrough, York, Leeds and Bradford over the previous six days in his route south.

I set out my stall: 'MND is not incurable, it has just been underfunded, and I have belief that by raising funds we can give the scientists and researchers the best possible opportunity to find that cure. We also need to help those living with MND, to give them hope and love so they know we are with them.'

I'd started out on this new long road in September, setting out into the unknown for my first ultra-marathon training stint. Seven hours later, I'd clocked up 66km. The next morning I rose at 4 a.m. and left for Leicester at 4.20 for a day's work. Answering the alarm call that morning was testing. We trained at Leicester, then it was home for a second go at an ultra, this time finishing at half past ten at night. That week Leicester gave me Wednesday and Friday at home, so I ran again on the Friday. Over those three days, I did a 66K, a 61K and a 62K. There was 9K of walking on each of the three days. That was what would get me through, I told myself. In an ultra you can walk small bits of it and strategise your running around those mini breaks.

Darrel Rogers joined me for half of the first day – he had a funeral to go to – and for all of the second and third days. Some of the conversations we had were just out there. Within those rambling chats there were some deep and meaningful words too. Darrel had become such a good friend, always by my side; and he had a knack of knowing what to say – and how to listen – through the ups and downs of our challenges. He would be my room-mate on the Ultra 7 in 7 and was an ideal companion to bounce thoughts and ideas off.

I realised: if I can get through three legs like this, after a five-hour car journey to Leicester and without the whole team driving us on, we can do the seven.

It was horrible, I won't pretend otherwise. People don't see the mental turmoil you go through. They turn on the telly and think – oh look, he's turned up and done this. If you told somebody to do three consecutive days of 61K-plus endurance . . . well, it's just horrible.

Already I could tell these ultras were going to empty my tank.

But somehow, when you've completed a leg, the fact that it was awful and that you've completed it regardless strengthens your belief that you can keep doing it day after day for as long as you have to.

To get yourself in a situation where you can run 60km, never mind back it up the next day, and the day after that, requires a lot more than running and walking every weekend to get yourself into acceptable shape. My knees weren't great going into that three-day training session, and they were a worry, but in the event they held up well. By then the vest with the sponsors' names on had been signed off. The figure raised at that point was £200,000 to £250,000, two weeks before the challenge was officially announced (in the end the initial sponsorship pool reached £298,000). So there was no going back on the commitment to run now, dodgy knees or not.

A committee of four was organising it: me, Phil Daly, Martin Wolstencroft and Peter Mackreth of the Carnegie School of Sport at Leeds Beckett. And we'd finalised how the money raised would be split. Ed Slater would be receiving part of it.

In August 2022, Ed, thirty-four years old, cycled from Gloucester to Leicester, then back again to the Kingsholm Stadium, a distance of 350 miles. Among those with him on the ride were the Gloucester players Billy Twelvetrees,

Lewis Ludlow and Fraser Balmain. A huge reception was waiting for him back at Kingsholm, where he said: 'I did have a cry when we came into Gloucester because a lot has changed for me since the diagnosis. I've had to give up rugby. I've had to give up a lot of things. A lot of this challenge was about proving I could still do something which was very difficult. It nearly broke me, but I got through it.'

It was Freddie Burns, who I worked with at Leicester, who had alerted me that Ed might have MND. I wanted to know how they knew, because Ed had been playing Premiership rugby the previous year. I was shocked. Freddie had bumped into him on holiday and Ed had shared the news. I told Freddie to send him my number in case he needed anything. Four days later Ed publicly confirmed his diagnosis.

Everyone at Leicester Tigers geared up to celebrate the finish of Ed's Gloucester-to-Leicester leg. What struck me right away was how quickly former team-mates came together, as they had in rugby league for Rob. Gloucester and Leicester had responded in a way reminiscent of how Leeds Rhinos had come to Rob's support. The camaraderie on Ed's challenge brought back all my memories of those early days of everyone rallying behind Rob. Although his cycle challenge was gruelling, you could see Ed had taken heart from people standing shoulder to shoulder with him.

I met him outside our ground. We were all staying that evening at the Hotel Brooklyn, adjacent to Welford Road, where I had an extra half hour with him. In the hotel Ed, his brother, some of the lads he'd cycled with and I talked about what he'd just achieved. I suggested the bike ride was one of the best things he could ever do. He looked at me as if I were crazy. Some of the other lads on his team had the glow my challenges had given me. Clearly they felt the same pride in helping a friend.

In August, too, Len Johnrose, the former footballer, had died. I was aware of Len working with the ninety-two Football League clubs, banging the drum for MND. It was a desperately sad day when he passed away.

September at least brought some brighter news for MND sufferers when scientists announced a treatment breakthrough. It applied only to 2 per cent of patients – those with the specific SOD1 genetic mutation – but had promising implications for others with the disease.

In late October I spoke to our nutritionist James Moran about how he saw the nutritional challenge on our ultras. Understandably James was inclined to approach it like a professional endurance event, but I was always conscious of the importance of morale on these challenges. The mood we're in is often determined by the food we eat, and the targets and rewards we set. There was give and take on both sides, as you'd expect when professionalism clashes with a charity event, where the overriding aim is to get from A to B.

I wanted to enjoy it, and if I was going to be eating plain pasta with tomato sauce every day I wouldn't enjoy it. I wasn't taking the challenge on as a professional cyclist or athlete. I needed to explain the importance of the team, and why I didn't want to be a cranky sod all week.

My fastest marathon times had been on the back of a McDonald's the night before. In professional sport for nineteen years I never went near a McDonald's before a game – or certainly not in the forty-eight-hour window before kick-off. Yet, the day before the 2017 Grand Final when Leeds played Castleford, I had a terrible cold, hadn't eaten all day and was doing the Yorkshire Marathon the following morning. I was at the game doing corporate work. On the way home I stopped for a McDonald's. The following day – smashed my marathon time.

Maybe it was the guilt, or perhaps the salt and sugar. Either way I did it a second time – and it worked again.

Food is so important. I felt better prepared going into the Ultra 7 in 7 eating what I wanted than I did the 101, even with all the science around it.

I was also conscious of not wanting spectators to see it as a professional event, a race against the clock. Oddly, the more you make it look like an event with times and speeds, the less goes in the collection pot.

When the time came for my training to taper, I expected to feel underdone. But that didn't trouble me, and, besides, I had no choice. I couldn't have cleared the diary to train full-time. I had a full-time job at Leicester to attend to. And anyway, I don't think I could have run any further or more intensively without getting injured. Those three days of

The lads joined me in Belfast at the BBC Sports Personality of the Year awards. Thankfully they were well behaved on the night . . . besides the 18ft Christmas tree coming down at the after-party.

ere I am receiving my MBE from ince William.

I met Prince Harry several times when he was patron of the Rugby Football League and in my time working there. After the Extra Mile he congratulated me for pulling together league and union.

Me with Leicester Tigers' head coach, Steve Borthwick, after the Premiership final win in 2022.

I had a rocky start with Leicester and rugby union, but thanks to the support of the team, m friends and family, I'm so glad I stuck with it.

he first challenge in 2020: seven marathons in seven days. We set out to raise £77,777, but ı the end we raised over £2 million.

he second challenge was to run 101 miles in twenty-four hours. Even in the middle of the ght, special people kept turning up to inspire us and give us the strength to go on.

The route for the seven ultras. We would run 60km per day for seven days from Murrayfield Stadium in Edinburgh to Old Trafford in Manchester.

Spot Martin with his stolen Scottish Saltire.

Running legend Steve Cram joined us for our second day. We were so ahead of schedule that he only reached us for the last 800m.

Day 5: turning up at York Minster felt like a Christmas film. Hundreds of wonderful people turned up to help us get where we needed to be.

always think, if you're going to put a pair of trainers on to run, they've got to make you ~~smile~~. The brighter the better.

~~Rob~~'s shirt number, 7, was always in our calculations when we set up the challenges. For the ~~Ultra~~ 7 in 7 Challenge we set our sights on raising £777,777.

We entered Old Trafford at half-time for the Rugby League World Cup. The whole Ultra 7 in 7 team came out onto the pitch, the crowd applauding, as Sally Nugent read out the total we'd raised so far: £1.3 million.

I told the crowd: 'If we can all try and be a bit of a better friend from time to time, I think we'll have a better place to live in.'

Rob and I at the BBC's *Sports Personality of the Year*, where Rob received the Helen Rollason Award.

Me and Rob running through the streets of Leeds, with him in the world's most high-tech wheelchair.

Day 6 of the Ultra 7 in 7 Challenge. Rob and I in front of the statue of Leeds legend, John Holmes, 'The Reluctant Hero'.

The Ultra 7 in 7 team waiting to make our entrance at Old Trafford. Exhausted but euphoric

Doddie Weir came to meet us at Murrayfield Stadium. It would be the last time I saw him. I'm honoured to have been able to call him a friend. He will always be a champion.

60K-plus runs helped enormously, especially the one where I was up at 4 a.m. to drive to Leicester, coach and come back, starting my run at 4 p.m. That was a true challenge on every level. I'd done two back to back as well, so I'd already proved one point to myself.

My big problem with the commuting was getting enough sleep. On the Friday before the Ultra 7 in 7, Leicester went down to Bath in the Premiership. We led 15–8 at half-time but lost 19–18 to a last-minute try by Bath's Will Butt. That didn't help my mood. We arrived home from Bath at 4 a.m. on the Saturday morning. Then it was a 7.30 start to get ready to leave for Edinburgh at noon. The team were gathering at the Dakota Hotel in Queensferry near the Scottish capital for a 7 a.m. Sunday start from Murrayfield. As I boarded the minibus in Saddleworth on Saturday morning to head north I felt quite leggy from lack of sleep.

Ahead of me lay 443km, or 276 miles, of road, at an average of around 40 miles a day.

We had plenty of sports science, a running vest with logos worth £20,000 each, and a new drum, which someone from the MND community would bang seven times each time we set off. The Leeds Rhinos website would show our exact location through a GPS tracker, so people could know when we would be at stops, and start and finish lines. We were well prepared. But we'd never tried anything on this scale. It was something of a mystery tour.

The Team Sheet for the Ultra 7 in 7

Runners

Kevin Sinfield
David Spencer – founder of Chartered Wealth
 Management
Chris Stephenson – sports industry CEO

Cyclists

Darrel Rogers – manager at the housing association
 Your Housing Group (YHG)
Martin Wolstencroft – co-founder and CEO of
 bar-restaurant operator Arc Inspirations (Banyan,
 The Box, Manahatta, etc.)
Phil Allingan – founder of Business Advice
 Services

Planning, logistics, medical and nutrition

Phil Daly – head of media and PR, Leeds Rhinos
Peter Mackreth – dean, Carnegie School of Sport,
 Leeds Beckett University
Professor Ben Jones – Leeds Beckett University,
 Research Lead Premiership Rugby, Performance and

214

Research Lead Rugby Football League, performance advisor to Leeds Rhinos

James Moran – performance nutritionist, Uno-X Pro Cycling Team, previously INEOS Grenadiers, British Cycling and English Institute of Sport

Gemma Phillips – NHS GP, Hull KR and England Rugby League

David O'Sullivan ('Dos') – founder of Pro Sport Physiotherapy in Huddersfield, former physio to England rugby league and rugby union teams at World Cups

MND Association

Jenn Scribbins PhD – regional fund-raiser for Yorkshire and Humberside, Motor Neurone Disease Association

Book co-author

Paul Hayward

Filming

Jimmy Bray – head of production, RAM Films
Joe Nisbett – lead videographer, RAM Films

Motorhome support

Chris Smith – motorhome owner and former town
  clerk
Glenn Milne – retired police officer

Guest runners/cyclists/attendees

Gemma Bonner, Alistair Brownlee, Steve Cram,
Jonathan Edwards, Matt Egan, Will Findlay, Brendan
Foster, Will Greenwood, Carl Hogg, Jamie Jones-
Buchanan, Richie Mathers, Jamie Peacock, Paul
Scholes, Beth Tweddle, Aled Walters

19

RUNNING THROUGH DODDIE'S WORLD

The night before it all began I told the team in a 6 p.m. meeting at our hotel in Queensferry: 'We're here for Rob, but Stephen, Doddie and Ed Slater have also become the band of brothers we represent.' The sportsmen with MND we were close to had grown in number and we would meet more people than ever with the disease across those 276 miles.

From the front of the room I looked out at the group we'd assembled for the toughest of our running challenges and was proud of the experts and friends who would set out at dawn the next day on the long road home. 'We have a great mix, young and old, male and female,' I told them. Then I added something new to the mix, calling everybody individually to the front to receive the shirt we would all wear, with a few words to each of them so they all knew they were valued.

I wanted them to feel how important they were to the

team. The night before many of the biggest sporting events there's a shirt presentation. It makes it special but also personal. Not everyone in our team would have experienced a shirt presentation. I also knew that our final, if you like, wasn't the next day. It would come at Old Trafford in seven days' time, when walking up the tunnel and on to the pitch at half-time would give people that sense of how it felt in high-level sport.

I told them a story about taking the recycling down to the bin store the night after that horrible loss to Bath in the last seconds of the game. I'd felt fairly crap about that. Grumpy. As I opened the recycling bins someone had put something in the wrong one – they'd put cardboard in the plastics. Lo and behold, it was a Ready Brek box, with its image of a glowing figure – a favourite emblem of mine. I came away from the bin store thinking: somebody's sending me a bit of a sign here.

The team was broadly the same one we'd used for the Extra Mile, with one or two additions. They were all friends. When you assemble the best people in their professions, and you have a spirit and a drive bonding them all, you can achieve amazing things.

Only one small cloud hung over the picture. England losing their Rugby League World Cup semi-final to Samoa that day was a setback for the country, and for us, in terms of the interest we might generate walking into Old Trafford the following Saturday. Australia v. Samoa wouldn't have the same capacity to raise the emotional charge. (Or so I thought. Seven days later passion was hardly lacking in the reception we received at the ground where Rob and I had played in so many Grand Finals.) I tried to reassure our Ultra team that England not being in the final wouldn't lessen the emotional impact of the fight against MND. I said: 'What is really special is what's in this room, and what will be with us on that day, with our families – and what we represent in the MND community.

'There are going to be some massive highs along the week. And there are going to be some lows. There will be some banter, there will be some people who are going to get cross and angry. I'll probably be the cranky one. Apologies in advance. None of it's personal. We're all here because we want to be. This could be one of the best weeks of your life.'

That was a bold claim to make about a challenge made up of early starts, long days, potentially filthy weather and multiple kinds of physical pain for the runners. But I meant it. And as you'll see in the account that follows, it wasn't a claim I had to retract.

We would break the days into three blocks: a first of 30km or so, then a short break with the morale boost of a bacon buttie and a brew, then smaller chunks, with the 1km walks incorporated later in the day.

Day 1 – Murrayfield to Melrose (13 November)

Just before 7 a.m. on the cold dark morning of Sunday 13 November a car pulled up at Murrayfield where people were gathered to send us on our way. In the passenger seat of the BMW was Doddie Weir, smiling through the windscreen. He was helped by his wife Kathy from the vehicle into his chair and joined us on the start line. The crowd sang 'Flower of Scotland' to get everyone in the mood.

We'd told Doddie he didn't need to be there because we expected to be seeing him the following morning in Melrose, at his home club. But he came anyway. Doddie was guest of honour at the Scotland–New Zealand game later that day to mark five years of his My Name'5 Doddie Foundation. The numbers on Scotland's shirts were in Doddie's blue and yellow tartan. It was an arduous day for him. His presence with us, though, left no room for doubt about why we were setting out on this massive expedition.

He'd had a rough few weeks – it was only when I saw him emerge from the car that I knew he'd be joining us. He was a very determined man. I could see in his eyes what it meant to him to be there. And it was special for each and every one of us.

Before Doddie made his entrance a few of us slipped away to lay a wreath at the Murrayfield war memorial. We stood beside the statue in the cold with our thoughts as the hub-bub around *BBC Breakfast's* live broadcast point grew in size and energy.

Others with MND were in the throng of supporters as the BBC did their usual brilliant job of broadcasting live from the set-off point. The mood was cheery, positive. You could sense that a big game was only hours away as the energy around the stadium began to build.

In the BBC's package, Rob, Stephen, Ed and Doddie sent messages of support. Rob called it 'the biggest challenge' of my life. He said via his Eye Gaze: 'I know you're putting your body on the line for your little mate but be very careful with it. I know you continue to push the boundaries of your body and I can't believe how you can do this for me and the suffering of MND. You're one of a kind mate and if everyone else had a friend like you the world would be a better place. Good luck pal. We trust in Kev.'

After Stephen and Ed (who wore a bright pink T-shirt, to match my trainers), Doddie had the last word: 'Kev, this is all for you. Good luck, we'll be watching.'

With the TV work complete, we braced ourselves for what was to come. David had picked up an injury in the Seven in Seven and Chris had caught Covid before the Extra Mile. But here we were at last. David is a wealth man-agement specialist and Chris a CEO. They weren't pro athletes. But the three of us were equal on that start line and would be equal still at the finish.

Seven bangs rang out from our new starting drum, hammered by a man called Bruce Atchison who'd done a phenomenal amount of work for Doddie's charity.

The light was coming up on a glistening Scottish morning as we jogged away from Scottish rugby's home into Edinburgh city centre, passing along the Royal Mile and on to the A7 towards Melrose Rugby Club, 62.9km on from where I'd given Doddie a hug outside Murrayfield. It was to be a deceptively calm and picturesque passage from that great city into Borders country, where Doddie and his family were so deeply rooted.

Clusters of supporters cheered us through every town and village and one woman handed Martin a Saltire to fly as he cycled behind us. Martin assumed it was his to keep. No chance. The lady later collared him in Melrose and asked for it back for a marathon she was going to run. He was sorry to see it go.

Everyone who comes out to cheer on these road trips has a story. On a high road on moorland three miles before our first stop a woman pulled over by herself in a remote layby to applaud. Her mother-in-law had died of MND and she'd studied the route in the hope of catching sight of us. She filmed us passing, to show her daughter, and called out 'It's amazing what you're doing!' as we struggled into a headwind. A private moment of remembrance for her, a small spur of encouragement for us. People shouting out might not realise that every word gave us strength.

And the kindness of strangers was apparent again at 11 a.m. when we stopped in a layby for the two-minute Remembrance Day silence, where Helen and Adrian White and Helen Brown, three local people, laid on bacon rolls, tea and coffee for twenty. As we pulled in, we were met by a face that looked familiar. It was Doddie's brother Tom, with his daughters, Doddie's nieces. Like Doddie, Tom is a farmer in the Blainslie area.

The Last Post played through Martin's music box. Then we turned left to continue the run to Melrose, and Tom turned right for Edinburgh to see the Scotland–All Blacks game. It feels haunting now to realise that when we spoke, Tom and all his family would soon be losing Doddie.

At the top of a hill a mum waited with her three children, who had painted a sign and sellotaped it to the side of a black Transit van, angled so we could see it. After we'd waved and passed, the children carefully unstuck the A4 sheets on which they'd painted the words.

I couldn't imagine the first day going better than it did. Blue sky, sun, only brief buffetings from the wind and an abundance of downhill stretches. A beautiful Scottish landscape passed our eyes. Driving gales and rain had been my expectation, it being November, this far north. A part of me had hoped for hostile conditions because it makes for better photographs and footage. The tougher people think it is, the more generous they are with donations. But for running we couldn't have asked for better weather, though I knew harder days were coming. Just before we stopped at a golf club about 40km in, I said to David, 'This route has been very kind to us, we've had a lot of down-hills today, that's why the speed has been consistent and quick.' But I knew the uphills were out there, waiting to hurt us.

It helped to know that, by design, each stage grew smaller and smaller. That's the way we set up the blocks. Mentally, as you go, you're knocking chunks off the challenge. The breaks were strategically placed. Blocks two and three passed faster than anticipated. I'd say on that first day we ran downhill for 50 of the 63Ks – a huge proportion.

We'd learned a lot from the Extra Mile the previous year. James and Ben were red hot on nutrition. It also helped that we all knew each other better. I was more comfortable saying about food 'I don't want that' or 'I don't like that'. From Edinburgh to Melrose I was completely comfortable with everything I ate and drank.

It's not good for me to run angry, and I didn't on that first day. The furthest I went down the path towards irritation was slight frustration when a bacon roll stop was further on than we expected – for perfectly good reasons to do with safe layby stops on busy roads.

Those short breaks aren't only about food and drink. They affect the morale of the group. When you're running and biking your mouth starts salivating as you approach a stop. It was nobody's fault that the stop was where it needed to be. You just don't see that at the time. You're in your own bubble of exertion and need.

Over 62.9km it feels like you're taking a hell of a lot of calories on, but you are burning a hell of a lot off. My watch told me I'd burned 5,200 calories, just from activity. You'd have to add 1,000 to that for just functioning. James had predicted a burn of 7,000 calories a day and that's about where we were when we pulled into Melrose.

Seven days of banter had begun, and it would barely pause this side of the finish in Manchester. Bruce Springsteen sang 'My Home Town' as we bounced into Melrose. That one was requested by the former Scotland international Carl Hogg, riding with us, who played for Leeds Tykes from 2003 to 2004 and whose wife Jill Douglas was president of Doddie's foundation. The song reminded me of my dad, who used to play it to me.

We ran into Melrose Rugby Club about an hour and ten minutes early and so caught a few people out. I tried to say hello later to those who arrived after we were already in ice baths or on massage tables. I didn't want anyone to miss out just because we had been ahead of schedule. The beauty of Melrose with its trees and surrounding hills was a suitably soothing place to end the day. Seven-a-side rugby was founded in the town in 1883 and every April still it's home to the Melrose Sevens.

Around the time we came to a halt at his old club, Doddie was being pushed by his sons on to the pitch for Scotland

v. the All Blacks. His trousers and scarf were blue and yellow tartan. On his feet were a pair of size 13 trainers in the same colours as mine.

There was a story attached to that . . .

As I said, brightly coloured trainers increase my urge to run, and my favourite ones are pink, though on the box it says 'rouge'. On one of the BBC Breakfast shows when the camera panned to my trainers Doddie made a comment about their pinkness. When Rob, Ed and Doddie went to do some filming Doddie was into me about these trainers. The next day, a text landed from him: 'Do you think you'll be able to get me those trainers? Size 13.'

Not easy. I went next best and found him some bright red ones, size 13. He was wearing them when he set us off at Murrayfield and again at the Scotland–All Blacks match, where the TV commentator reeled off the numbers: £8 million raised by Doddie's foundation. All thirty players came over to applaud him and the Murrayfield crowd clapped him to the skies.

Jamie Ritchie, Scotland's captain, said after the game: 'It's bigger than rugby, but we did that for Doddie, such a special man. We're glad we could put a decent performance out there for him, but sorry we couldn't get the result. I don't think anything defines brave more than Doddie. We were so proud that we could wear his tartan on our back.'

The love expressed for him across Scotland made it even more poignant for us to return that evening to the Melrose clubhouse for a Q & A. Doddie's sister Kirsty was in the room. You could feel the history and communal spirit of the club. By then the Melrose Community 7 in 7 Challenge team were endeavouring to cover collectively the same number of miles we'd be taking on.

I told them the story of how a '5ft 4in guy and a guy who was 6ft 10in' had bonded on the day they met to discuss the terrifying fate they were both facing – the day the 'friendly giraffe', as Rob called him, became my old team-mate's MND mentor.

In the gallery of international players produced by this remarkable Borders club was a photograph of G. Weir – George Weir, to give him his official name – fresh-faced and beaming beneath a Scotland cap.

Introducing us to the Melrose audience, the compere described the challenge we'd taken on as 'pretty impossible', which brought a rueful smile to the faces of Chris and David.

I talked about all the fund-raising work being done by all the MND-related groups around the country. 'It's the greatest gift when you can provide hope for people,' I said. And I spoke a lot about our whole operation and how everyone in our team was inter-dependent. We were all there to meet the audience. On all seven nights we went out to eat as a group. Nobody stayed in their room or went off to eat elsewhere. Every evening we wanted to be in one another's company, sharing thoughts on the day behind us and cranking it up for the day ahead.

I said to the audience in Melrose: 'Great teams just work, don't they?'

Day 1 had been a triumph that allowed the new members to bed smoothly into the team. The Saturday night pre-start meeting had been excellent too. Both enabled us to work out how the various personalities would fit together. More and more as the days became more draining we'd need that togetherness.

From Melrose to Otterburn I knew the hills would become steeper and the weather less hospitable. At the Melrose Q & A Keith Robertson, who won forty-four caps for Scotland, asked what would stop us completing all seven ultras. 'The only thing that will stop us is a serious injury,' I replied. 'I can't control that. I can't fix it. What I can ensure is that I have the best team around the three of us; the best team who physically, mentally and emotionally give us what we need. Snap an Achilles tendon and . . . even then, I think the three of us would still try.

'It matters. This matters. This isn't just three lads going for a 10K run. People need to see us finish, otherwise the money won't come in. And if we don't get the money in, we can't find a cure.'

Day 2 – Melrose to Otterburn (14 November)

Not long after we'd left Melrose behind a white-coated man stepped out of Martin Baird's butcher's shop and approached members of our team who were loading bags to take them on to the next stop. In his hand was a big bag of pies and sausage rolls. 'These are for you all on your journey,' he said. 'Doddie is a friend of mine.' Then he turned and walked back towards the brightly lit window of his shop.

Martin Baird's offerings were added to our stockpile of fuel. And the team members who'd spoken to him drove away from Melrose with another example of the kindness that was enveloping us.

The story of day 2 was the hills – the things we'd avoided on day 1 but could no longer dodge. Large parts of the route from Melrose to Otterburn in Northumberland were barren. But we saw people scattered everywhere in the middle of nowhere. The climb to the border was hefty. We played a fair bit of 'Flower of Scotland' on the route but as soon as we crossed the border 'Jerusalem' was on, and a bit of 'Land of Hope and Glory'. Just to amuse ourselves.

It was grey and misty on the ascent to Carter Bar, the high monument that acts as a border post on the eastern side of those two countries. To the north sits the battle site of Redeswire Fray. Below the summit you head for the Whitelee nature reserve and the long Catcleugh Reservoir.

The vast bulk of the run from Carter Bar was downhill, and it was those descents that gave me the first hint of gip in my quads, the four muscles found in the front of your thighs. It's a myth that downhills are what runners dream of. As I said, walks of 1km are factored into ultra-marathons. Everybody says you should use those up on the hills, to take pressure off, but to protect your body it's sometimes wiser to walk downhill. The problem is, your mind is telling you that would be daft.

By the end of the second day my quads were sore. In the village hall we stopped at for our first refreshment stop of the day I was in need of support from our physio David O'Sullivan, or Dos as we call him. My knees had been painful for around a year. The quads can compensate by taking the load off the knees. Working away in that remote village hall, Dos was trying to maintain tendon health – again, on the basis that downhill was where the damage might be done.

We knew Steve Cram was due to join us up ahead. The 1983 world champion and 1984 Olympic silver medallist in the 1,500m was a luxury addition to our group, but we weren't shown up for long. For the second day we were significantly ahead of schedule. Through no fault of his we were only 800 or so metres from the finish when Steve joined us. I'd dropped him a message to say we were going to be up in his neck of the woods and straight away he'd agreed to join us. Steve said he was 'embarrassed' to have run for such a short time, but he didn't need to be. The following day he was back for more.

A constant headache of such long runs is traffic management, which worked like this. The three cyclists rode in front of or behind the three runners and swapped positions to block the wind and keep the convoy tight. Just behind us was the control van driven by Pete Mackreth, who had to maintain the correct distance and wave traffic around our little peloton. It's a stressful job to be doing seven hours a day, especially on busy A-roads when traffic is building up.

As a runner you're aware of this constant flow of engines and exhaust fumes. You can hear the revving of the van behind you and when an HGV comes flying past you really know about it. You're only a metre or two away from this juggernaut that's flying up behind you. If it hit you it would crush you – crush all of us. The bikers did a fine job of controlling the whoosh of cars, vans and lorries, and of making sure we didn't cause five-mile tailbacks with our slow-moving phalanx.

Every motorist over those first two days was forgiving of the congestion we sometimes created. But whenever people weren't aware of what we were up to, we did encounter the odd flash of annoyance. As we headed out of Scotland, a police car flew past us and stopped in a layby up ahead. Oh no, I thought, what have we done wrong? But the team told me later the woman officer inside was lovely. She just wanted to see us, and even asked one of our support staff not to tell her bosses they'd seen her make a detour to cheer us on.

There was a new outside influence guiding me: Rob Pope (Rob P from now on), an extraordinary extreme distance runner from Merseyside, who ran five complete crossings of America. His guiding light was the fictional Forrest Gump, played in the film by Tom Hanks.

Rob Burrow and I have a mutual friend, a doctor who used to be at the Rhinos, John Power, a Liverpudlian who went to school with Rob P. John asked if he could put me in touch with him. Brilliant, I said. We swapped numbers and missed each other about ten times with phone calls before we finally spoke six weeks before the Ultra 7 in 7.

Rob P told me that to make life easier I needed to do a particular stretching exercise, and talked about time – how slow we ought to go. He emphasised that we weren't trying to break world records, only to get from A to B. Nobody would care, Rob P said, how quickly we ran the seven ultra-marathons. His estimate was that about 1 per cent of people in the world would know how fast an ultra ought to be run. The vast majority of spectators are oblivious. They just want to know you made it through.

Great advice – because a part of me is so competitive with myself. Trying to change my view on how quickly we covered the ground was going to be important in ensuring we actually completed the challenge. All the fund-raising hung on that.

We ran hard in the first block, but were smarter after that, to buy time and spend more of it with people at the stops. Rob P texted me after day 2 to say well done and to remind me about the pace. 'Simple long sleeves, leggings with breathable jacket, will see you through the week,' he wrote. 'Just have a couple of spare long sleeves and make sure you dry the jacket off. Turn it inside out during dry spells. If you stop to eat and have a dry top, whack that on before you eat. Resting in wet clothes gets old quickly. You've got this, dude.'

Rob P's strongest message was: if you feel like stopping, stop. He recalled halting in a Subway sandwich shop in America for ninety minutes, having a foot-long sub, watching the world go by, then getting back out there. The one area where I still had to fight my headstrong urges was in the first 30Ks, to put the worst behind us. But Rob P's message was always in my head.

After 2,755ft of climbing, and 2,555ft of descent, we finished at 2.40 p.m. Rob Burrow, Doddie, Ed and Stephen all texted me after that second leg. They were all watching it, following our progress.

We stayed at Otterburn Castle, where we were treated like royalty. As we entered, a local Geordie man with the usual Tyneside fondness for Kevin Keegan shouted, 'You're the second King Kev we've had in this region!' Then he remembered our illustrious guest was a Sunderland fan and added, 'Steve Cram won't like that. He's a Mackem.'

Every person who turned out, on every road and in every layby, had a reason for being there, a connection, often with MND but sometimes just with us, as fund-raisers. In each and every instance we were appreciative. At each stop trying to spend time with people was complicated. I wanted to sit down, have something to eat, go to the toilet. But I was always conscious there were eyes on us, and it was important to say a short hello, have pictures taken, and speak to the gathering, which I always did.

I never left a stop without thanking people for coming out. It's not fair, not right, to leave without saying that. I knew that by day 5 or 6 it would become very difficult to maintain my energy for talking to huge groups of people, but I was determined to try my best to keep doing it. A couple of words or a photograph have a lasting effect on people who are there because they've lost someone to MND.

Their presence gave us fuel. When we looked across the UK, bad news kept coming. When you put a news channel on, as I did in Otterburn, you saw how tough life was for everybody. People were perhaps taking something from the BBC coverage of our efforts, and maybe thinking: 'The world int that bad. You can see the good in people.'

20

THE LIGHTS OF YORK MINSTER

Day 3 – Otterburn to Chester-le-Street (15 November)

Of the three Ultra 7 in 7 runners I was the only ex-professional sportsman, but the courage and resilience shown by my companions was indispensable. From the first step I was adamant that we'd start as a team and finish as one. Our backgrounds didn't matter. We were in this together.

Both Chris and David are remarkable in different ways. Chris, who's fifty-two, is the main reason I started to run seriously. He was often the driver, saying, 'Do you fancy doing London?' or 'I can get us into this or that event.' I could never draw from Chris a clear sense of how much he'd trained, but for him to do what he did on the Ultra 7 in 7 was incredible. His relationship with Martin, our shop steward, was a bit love-hate, but it was pleasing to see Chris become such good friends with everyone on the team. I know how much it meant to him.

David became a friend after his wife Erin and Jayne met at fitness classes. Not long after I finished playing, Jayne said, 'I've booked us a holiday. We're going to Mexico. With David and Erin.'

I said: 'Who's David and Erin?'

But we just hit it off. David loves training and is immensely positive. When I asked him whether he fancied being involved in the Seven in Seven he replied with one word: 'Yeah.' And from there he was tied into it all. I know how hard he trained for the ultras too. He gave up drinking for months, which will have been hard, because he likes a beer. He bought seven pairs of trainers, one for each day, although he didn't use them all.

Many people who have taken on extreme challenges will be able to see in David and Chris their own struggles to achieve remarkable feats. They're very relatable. I needed them both. They helped me massively, probably without knowing just how much they kept me going when things turned tough.

By now the elements were stacking up against us. This northern winter landscape was never going to let us run through it laughing and singing the whole way.

On one particularly barren stretch of moorland a farmer appeared at a small turn-off. Inhabitants of remote farm-houses and small rural communities would often appear and stand next to working Land Rovers, waiting patiently for a sight of us approaching. This farmer saw us fighting through sheeting rain and remarked to two of our team: 'The bleakest part of the day, this.' Later the terrain became more pleasing on the eye, but the drabness continued until we turned up dripping in Chester-le-Street. The soft rain of the morning turned to a drumbeat, slackening off only as we made our way up the hills of Newcastle city centre to an MND event at Banyans – a good meal and a U2 tribute band, attended by some of the regional staff of the MND Association.

Not long after that grim pronouncement by the farmer a car pulled to a halt on the opposite carriageway and out jumped Steve Cram for a second shift. Allison Curbishley, Steve's partner, had tracked us down on the GPS and delivered Steve for another run. This one was longer. We said our goodbyes in a layby beside Kirkharle Lake and ploughed on without a world-class runner for everyone to photobomb.

At Kirkwhelpington for our 8.30 a.m. stop, the schoolchildren appeared with three huge painted boards, each with a number 7 on it. A lady stepped forward with a large Tupperware box full of flapjacks she'd baked that morning. A couple said they had driven for an hour and a half to be there.

Lorry drivers honked their horns as they passed. Those at the wheel of HGVs seemed to have a special affection for us, even though we sometimes held them up when it was impossible for them to overtake. The day's dream stop was the bacon sarnies we knew we'd get at the Tomahawk Steakhouse near Ponteland.

The foulness of wet November weather was now pummelling us. But the villagers of Belsay would never have guessed we were being battered by the elements. In honour of Phil Daly, who's a Liverpool fan, we piled through Belsay belting out 'You'll Never Walk Alone', swinging our arms and punching the air, to the bemusement of the locals. Music, camaraderie and food were our fuel. At dinner later that wild rendition of the Anfield anthem was confirmed as the high point of the day.

After Ponteland, we were on our way to two great Newcastle venues. First Kingston Park, home of Newcastle Falcons, nearly 44km into the day's run. After six years at Melrose, Doddie played ninety-seven times for the Falcons from 1995 to 2002. Jonny Wilkinson, Gary Armstrong and Alan Tait were team-mates. Doddie won the 1998 Premiership title there and captained the side that won the 2001 Anglo-Welsh Cup before joining the new Scottish regional side Border Reivers. The whole Falcons team were there to support us, along with Lee Wilkinson and Ian Donaldson, two guys with MND I enjoyed talking to.

A very nice woman at Kingston Park said of me: 'He makes it look so easy, he looks like he's just strolling to the shops.' I can assure her, appearances can deceive.

Then, St James' Park, Newcastle United's ground, where we slowed to a halt at the players' entrance in the Milburn Stand. 'Local Hero' – another club anthem – was playing to an enthusiastic crowd. And another great north-eastern runner and friend of Steve Cram was waiting at the top of the steps.

Brendan Foster was chancellor of Leeds Beckett University when I graduated and presented me with my certificate. Now I was wrapped in a hug with him. Soon I would be on the St James' Park pitch with him and the Rugby League World Cup trophy. Brendan's office was on the other side of the Tyne Bridge and he said he'd get his staff out after we'd taken soup and sandwiches and fought our way towards Durham County Cricket Club at Chester-le-Street.

But he didn't warn us about the pools of water on the bridge and the waves these would send crashing over us as heavy vehicles powered through the standing water. Martin, who had the music box strapped to his bike, was particularly delighted with these drenchings. It was too comical to get upset about. It was also on that leg that Chris was pushed into thorn bushes and Phil ended up like 'a turtle on its back', in Martin's words, after falling off his bike. So if the journey so far sounds smoothly professional – and serious – it wasn't always.

In the very last section before the cricket club we got horribly lost and ended up doubling back through a series of neighbourhoods in search of the right path. A family who observed us going back and forth insanely said 'it was like watching a Benny Hill sketch'.

We were to see that family at the finish line and again the next morning. We shared with them an exchange the team will never forget.

Day 4 – Chester-le-Street to Stokesley (16 November)

Standing by the gates of Durham's home ground at 6.45 a.m. was eight-year-old Harriet Taylor, daughter of Mike and Andrea. At the finish the previous day I'd given Harriet the snood I used as a headband. It was wet with rain and sweat but I figured Mike and Andrea would soon have it in the washing machine.

In the dark the next day, Harriet was back with the snood, now clean and dry. She also came with a story to tell. She'd seen Rob's daughters Macy and Maya in the recent BBC documentary and had told her parents 'we need to do something to help'. It was the example of Macy's love and courage for Rob that had inspired her. And her mum told us that Harriet would be running 1km before school as a show of solidarity. It was a beautiful reminder of how kindness can spread.

When I gave the snood to Harriet I understood the value of what I was doing. It was rooted in my ballboy days at

Oldham, when I'd collect tie-ups from the pitch. That was how I learned what those small totems could mean, and how long the effect of a small interaction can last, because that was my experience as a kid, when I was awed by the adult world.

As Harriet headed off for her run, I felt a sharp sense of entering unknown territory. In training I had only run three times at 60km or more. Now I was facing a fourth leg at that kind of distance for the first time in my life. And these were back to back.

The target now was the North Riding Football Association in Stokesley, via Middlesbrough, where our tour of big stadiums would continue at the Riverside. Running to the Wynyard Estate, we found ourselves on a track that was billed as a cycle route but was more like a bridlepath. 'I've never seen so much horseshit in my life,' was Martin's verdict, and once more there was irritation laced with humour. The conversations at the next stop removed any right to moan about a detour.

In a pub called the Stables we found Jackie Bradburn, who had MND, with her friends Sonia Henman, whose husband had died of MND, and Anne Salway. Jackie was keen to talk to us, and quite tearful. As we came in, Jackie said to those around her: 'There are no words . . .'

In the warmth, while everyone buzzed around, Jackie wanted to show us a photograph. It was her with Doddie, in his kitchen. She'd been to see him for encouragement.

Jackie was quite overwhelmed. I stroked her back and tried to console her. I said as gently as I could, 'You'll set me off too.'

We were so sorry to hear early in January 2023 that Sonia Henman had died suddenly on New Year's Eve.

The stories people tell you all cut through, and they stay with you. Further down the road, outside Middlesbrough's ground, I met a lady I'd seen on the news – Cath Muir – with a breathing apparatus. Some people show you the brutal side of the disease. Breathing devices are among the most striking symbols of the damage MND can do. The more tired you are from running, the more emotional you become when those with MND and their families start welling up. I choked up talking to Cath. That's a brave woman there. I hoped that what we were doing would encourage more like Cath to come out and enjoy their lives as best they could.

Middlesbrough Football Club looked after us royally. They too had an MND connection. Willie Maddren had played 293 times for the club between 1969 and 1979 and managed Boro for two years in the mid-eighties. He was diagnosed with MND in 1995 and raised £200,000 for research. Willie died at a hospice in Stockton-on-Tees aged forty-nine. We were proud to step on to the Riverside pitch to be photographed with a signed Boro shirt. Martin was knocked over in the jostle for the photo and became the draught excluder at our feet.

As always, I used those encounters to drive me on. Just as in the Seven in Seven I remember often being ready to cry, the Ultra 7 in 7 was both physical and emotional. There are so many people telling you that their father died of MND, their grandfather was taken away by it. A man had told me at the previous night's function: 'My son got it at thirty-one and passed away within fifteen months.' He was an ultra-runner who tried to climb Kilimanjaro, got so far up, but couldn't use his arms. He died not long afterwards. His mother and father went to the mountain as a pilgrimage, with the same sherpas.

There is this stat that 5,000 people have MND at any one time. But that can blind you to the countless cases there were previously – the thousands who'd already been through it. A lot of the families of those departed people had to sit with their trauma. It wasn't really known what MND was; some people who contracted it felt shame about their condition. Now, those left behind can express the emotional pain they endured. That's where Rob has been a shining light for the MND community. He's given a sense of safety to a lot of people who might previously have locked the doors and closed the curtains.

Together we were moving the dial – that was the big thing. What we could do in the here and now was to make sure people could have better lives. We'd seen Rob lose the ability to communicate with his kids, and the boost it gave him to get it back through his Eye Gaze. It restored him to being a fully-fledged member of the family rather than a guy sat silently in the corner, which is how he might have felt.

Stokesley was another demonstration of how our journey was gaining force, drawing bigger and bigger crowds, spreading the word. Once again we pulled to a halt earlier than scheduled. I said a few words, then dived inside for an ice bath and a recovery session with Dos. I thought the day was over.

But through the door came Phil. 'You're probably going to need to come outside again,' he said.

'No problem,' I said, 'I'll be out in a while.'

'No, no, the crowd's tripled,' Phil said. 'There's an unbelievable number of people out there.'

Curious but still not flustered, I showered, dried myself and put some clothes on.

As we left the building, Phil told me there was a box to stand on and a microphone waiting for me.

'I need a microphone? Are there that many people here?'

Stepping on to the box, I could see this mass of people stretching across the car park.

'I don't ask any of you to run seven ultras at all, but there is a but in this,' I told them. 'If you can all just do a little bit for the person next to you, we'll have a better place to live in.'

As I told Jimmy and Joe for the *Ultra 7 in 7* documentary: 'I never expected when we set out that at any point I'd be standing on a box with a microphone in my hand, speaking to people and ensuring they understood what we were trying to do. And they did. They really did. That made me proud.'

Day 5 – Stokesley to York (17 November)

The rain was drumming on the roof as we fumbled into pitch darkness to run one of the longest legs of the challenge. You got soaked just running from the annex where our hotel rooms were to the breakfast area. And you could get wet too sleeping under Martin's room. The previous night he had run a bath and not noticed the water slipping over the tub's edge and through the ceiling of the room I was sharing with Darrel. He was in the doghouse for that. But it gave us another running joke.

There was laughter too at the sheer horribleness of the conditions. And some trepidation. The wonderful staff at the North Riding FA were waiting for us again at their clubhouse. There was no way the BBC could have filmed outside in such conditions so we huddled in the clubhouse. Once again it was the BBC's John Maguire revving up the crowd and updating the *Breakfast* audience on our mission. The bar was crammed. Amazingly, a throng of people had braved the elements to send us off and surged forward to force tenners and twenties into our collection buckets.

Even with Jamie Peacock and mates from Leicester Matt Egan, Will Findlay and Aled Walters joining us, this was always going to be the hardest day – 72km – and it was absolutely hammering it down from the minute we set off. Throughout the build-up we'd spent a lot of time negotiating with local authorities about where we could and couldn't go. On this leg we had to add an extra few kilometres to avoid a high-speed section of the A19.

Thirsk Garden Centre was an intensely emotional stop. We saw Cath Muir again waiting inside among people shopping for the usual gardening gear. Life went on as normal for them as our mad gang of runners, cyclists and helpers commandeered a section of the café for the recovery, and to see Sally Nugent, who'd been staying nearby.

We were looked after by the café manager, Shirley Clarkson, whose father died of MND when she was young. Shirley was shaking as she spoke to members of our team. It was all flooding back for her.

In one corner of the café David was explaining how he managed to stay so positive and open-hearted on such a gruelling trial of the spirit. 'It's a mindset – positivity or negativity,' he said. 'It's habitual.' But was he really positive all the time about running so far, and for so long? 'I try to be,' he said.

By now Jenn Scribbins from the MND Association was collecting so much money that she needed a police escort to go to the bank. And soon we'd be running into a magical scene at York Minster, where Christmas lights were already hanging from trees and students were celebrating their graduation that afternoon inside the Minster.

First, though, there was a surprise waiting for me at Craig Lidster's horseracing yard at Easingwold, which didn't appear where our calculations had said it would – we were 4km out. And we were drenched and freezing. We'd been on our legs for six or seven hours. Round every corner we'd hoped to see those stables but they were start-ing to feel like a mirage. Even when we found them we'd still have 20K to run to reach York – practically a half marathon.

Despair was starting to nibble at us. But waiting for us there were Jayne and Chris and David's wives, Alex and Erin. Jayne and I hugged, and kissed, and stayed hugging for a long time. All the sacrifices I'd made at home raced round my mind. The boost to our morale was huge. Our time together was fleeting, but enough to connect me to Jayne and the boys and renew my energy.

As the streets narrowed on our run into the old heart of York, the pavements were crammed with people cheering and shouting us on. As we waved and smiled back we were engulfed by their goodwill. And we couldn't comprehend the scene at York Minster, where hundreds had gathered to greet us. As I told the MND Association's podcast: 'It was around four o'clock, the Christmas lights were on, it had just started to get a little bit dark . . . It was just

247

surreal, like something out of a Charles Dickens film, a Christmas film. There were so many wonderful people there to see us, it was emotional for all the team – and certainly for myself. The team just knitted together wonderfully, and people went above and beyond. They were so selfless to make sure the runners and cyclists got where we needed to be. The banter, the laughter and the support was brilliant, and it's the best team I've ever been in.'

The spirit by the end of that leg was as good as it had been all week because we knew we'd got the most difficult day out of the way. We'd travelled just over 200 miles in five days. Sure, there was wear and tear. I told the crowd in York: 'If I can never run again after Saturday, I'm not bothered.'

We were elated, but drained. We knew we'd have to scrap and fight again to get it done. But the team would get us through. I had no doubt whatsoever.

That evening we reconvened at Manahatta, a New York-inspired bar-restaurant in York, for an MND event. Jamie Jones was on the mic. He spoke to the crowd about 'our comrade and brother, Rob'.

It was so good to have Jamie alongside us. As I said in Melrose: 'When you need someone to make a five-metre carry close to your try-line, sometimes you look around and there aren't many takers, are there? Jamie Peacock and Jamie Jones – every time it would be "give me the ball". They're unbelievable men.'

Jamie asked me what the worst moment was so far, and I owned up to it. 'There have been moments where I've thought "I don't need this",' I said, 'but because we had such a great team it just gets fixed.' The team members were so good in their professions – nutrition, medical, logistics – that they were constantly thinking several steps ahead.

I told the people in Manahatta: 'What I saw coming into York was incredible. I'd never seen anything like that. I'm fortunate to have been in some wonderful teams who won Challenge Cups and Grand Finals and all sorts, but I don't think I've ever had a reception like that. You've given us a very special moment and a memory that will stick with us for the rest of our lives.'

I thought of Ed Slater, the only one in our group we wouldn't have a chance to visit, and commented: 'Unfortunately we've run out of days to run to Gloucester, and it's too far.'

With bedtime approaching I returned to my message: 'What Rob has been able to do is become a beacon for the MND community, and I like to think we've helped it shine a bit brighter this week.'

I also told the audience about the variety of stories we'd heard. A person saying she lost someone thirty years ago from it; another saying their husband had died three weeks back – all of them willing to share that now, and proud to share it, though they were teary. We took enormous energy and inspiration from those testimonies.

Martin had arranged the venue again and I called him 'our energy giver'. With a caveat: 'He does have his moments. He flooded our bedroom when his bath over-flowed. He wasn't on my Christmas card list last night.'

Another emotional day lay ahead. We'd be running to Headingley, where Rob would be waiting, then to Bradford City, knowing that Stephen Darby would be there. Before heading back to the hotel for some desperately needed sleep, I suggested to the audience that you don't have to run 60km in a day to change the world, 'There's always a small way you can help the person next to you.'

Survival: sports science – and Jaffa Cakes

By now I'd settled into a regimen of preparation, nutrition and recovery. This is how it worked . . .

I'd get up and stretch. The legs don't want to run when you get up after two or three ultras back to back. Calves, hamstrings and particularly quads, which bear the brunt, all grumble. I used the Rob Pope stretch a couple of times. It's very close anyway to a professional sport mobility stretch. It's a good one.

Then breakfast, typically of a slice of toast with marmalade and a cup of coffee.

Then I'd climb on to Dos's physio table to make sure my quads were at full length. Then he would work on my tendons, ham-strings, the backs of my knees. The muscles are important but the downhills mess with the tendons.

After a couple of days I fell into a pattern of being worked on by Dos at every major stop. I was bruised from it. When you stop playing you don't really do soft tissue work so if you put anyone off the street on that physio bed they would be bruised. You get conditioned to it.

Food wise, a constant stream of Maurten to drink. It's designed with a perfect ratio of glucose and fructose. The marathon runner Kipchoge uses it. I also had electrolyte drinks – not too often, but they were my go-to, as they were on the Extra Mile, when I knew I needed them. James Moran was brilliantly flexible. I asked him for loads of flapjacks and Jaffa Cakes. I must have had a hundred Jaffa Cakes in the first four days alone. Then fifteen halves of flapjack. At every food break we'd be dipping in.

I was burning around 7,500 calories each day. The constant drinks, flapjacks and Jaffa Cakes were helpful. Then you'd have the bacon butties and a brew – for morale. That's just to give everyone a lift. There's no nutritional value in it.

My weight after four days hadn't changed at all. The night before I had two starters, two mains and a dessert, and felt stuffed. But I woke the following morning and was the same weight I'd been all along.

You tend to put weight on during the running because you're taking so much on, but in the morning you're back where you should be.

It would be easy to under-budget and not have as much. I was almost force-feeding myself. I ate a lot more than I thought I would.

251

You might wonder how a pro diet for seven ultras would differ from a fund-raising one. I don't think a pro diet would stretch to the flapjacks, but James was quite happy for me to have them, for the long-burning carbs in the oats. A lot of athletes would have porridge in the morning. James would probably lean more towards rice cakes. Jelly babies are used by a lot of athletes, but I'd rather not have them, for the sake of my teeth.

I drank a lot of recovery shakes. And at the end of a leg I would have an ice bath and haul myself on to the physio table. You can do it either way round, but if you have the physio first you avoid spending twenty minutes shivering on the bed.

I also used a machine called Normatec, which is basically two inflatable tubes that you put your legs in. It inflates around your feet, then the next section up, then the next one, so it pushes all the toxins up towards your lymph nodes and clears, to stop some of the swelling. I did thirty minutes of that after dinner, then went to bed, in tubigrip. Compression pants were another option, but I found the tubigrip more comfortable. Compression pants are too tight on your privates.

At the end of an ultra, Dos would do a 'flush' to my muscles to try to clear some of the rubbish out. It's not just the lactic acid but pooling of fluid, pooling of crap blood. He'd also look to get rid of any knots and try to ensure a really good blood flow. The reason he's so good is he doesn't hold back. He never has. That's why I was bruised. But without him damaging me the runs would have inflicted far more havoc. I always felt better after I'd been in with him.

With the 5 a.m. starts and 7 a.m. send-offs I didn't get enough sleep. As I've outlined, on some of the evenings there were additional fund-raising functions. We had the U2 tribute band in Newcastle and in York on the Thursday night we had that significant function lined up in Manahatta. I knew we had a big day the following day, the Friday. I was happy to do a Q & A at 8 p.m. in York but I knew I'd need to be away an hour after it began.

The 7 a.m. BBC Breakfast start made it a very early wake-up but it tied in with Rob's number, so I had no problem with it, especially after everything the BBC had done for us. Ideally you would start the next day where your hotel is, or be very close. James told the MND Matters podcast after day 5: 'He's better than he was in the Extra Mile challenge. His body's battered, but he's OK.'

21

EMBRACING ROB AND STEPHEN

Day 6 – York to Bradford City FC
(18 November)

Throughout the week we and all the people who worked with us took on board a lot of intense emotion from the families we met along the way. The stories stuck in our hearts and were carried right across the northern half of Britain. For me, the feelings that had been building up spilled out the day we ran to Headingley to see Rob Burrow and then to Bradford to meet up with Stephen Darby. Both times tears broke whatever resistance I had left.

Off we went, from that beautiful scene at York Minster – it was crowded again – past the racecourse on the Knavesmire towards Tadcaster. Now I could feel Leeds and Headingley in the air. I've mentioned that our run wasn't always a smooth parade. There were wrong turns and frictions. On one stop we mislaid the drum and had to hit a life-sized plastic cow seven times instead. And we knew there would be tensions with motorists. But we didn't expect to be in combat the way we were on day 6.

Running uphill, we noticed a car jamming on its brakes to avoid another one that had tried to go round us. The driver who'd slammed his foot on the brakes then looked to swerve round us. Martin tried to slow him down, but this guy simply opened his door as Martin tried to pass and knocked him off his bike. Then he sped off in pursuit of the rest of us. Alistair Brownlee had just joined us on the run. Jamie Jones had to resist the urge to throw something at the crazy driver, who paid a small price for his anger when Darrel nearly collided with him and knocked his wing mirror off. Whatever his problem was, it was obviously getting the better of him.

The rest of the day was road rage free. I could prepare myself for the moment I would run through those Headingley gates for a reunion that was bound to overwhelm not just me but many in the team and in the crowd.

And before long there he was, still, silent and patient, under John Holmes's statue which commemorated 'The Reluctant Hero', born in Kirkstall, veteran of 625 games for Leeds and nineteen major finals, holder of fourteen winners' medals and World Cup winner in 1972 with Great Britain. Holmes loomed over Rob – two giants of the club together.

Rob doesn't bring his Eye Gaze to public events so in

those situations there are no words from him, only his eyes and his smile. I found myself talking to him and hoping to hear something back. And I knew I wasn't going to get it. That was painful. Lindsey and Rob's parents Geoff and Irene were there too, and you could see the distress in Geoff. For all of us, to run in and see Rob waiting like a patient old friend, with all those eyeballs on him, cut straight through.

Privacy would have been my preference, a chance for us to connect in our own space, but I understood that wasn't possible. It needed to be public for everyone to see and understand the magnitude of the cause we were running for.

The battle inside me was to stay strong but at the same time not hide my feelings. I didn't want the audience to see a blubbering mess. It didn't seem like a good idea either for Rob to see me wrecked by the sight of him. That could only make it harder on his side. It wouldn't have been fair to load my feelings on to him.

I lowered my head to embrace Rob and to say a few personal words, and just as I did so the bench coat Lindsey had rolled over my back and shoulders fell forward over my head, enclosing Rob and me in a kind of mini tent. People might have thought I pulled the coat over us on purpose, to create a private space, but I didn't.

Standing by Rob's side, I began to address the crowd, but couldn't go on, and lowered my hands to my knees. If I double over, you know I'm crying. I didn't want to make eye contact with anyone because I knew it would make me cry even more. Lowering my head in a place where Rob couldn't see me took that away. I straightened up, looked out at the waiting faces and made myself continue. I told the crowd: 'We'll find a cure for this disease, all right? I don't know when, but we all keep fighting together. We'll get there.'

Inside the stadium I then had a second chance to speak to Rob. Again I lowered my head close to his and said, 'I'll text you later on. I'm OK, mate, just so you know. Quads are a bit tight. Achilles is a bit sore. It only started hurting today. I'm all right, mate. We'll get it done, all right?'

Jayne had told me Jack would be there and I found him waiting for me near Rob, inside the South Stand. That was another reunion that was bound to make me emotional because I hadn't seen my sons for a week. None of us had seen our kids. The Rhinos first-team squad were also all there. That too meant a lot.

Waking up that Friday, the first thing I'd said to Darrel was that I couldn't wait to watch Sam play football on the Sunday morning, when we were all home. I saw Jayne on Thursday and Jack on Friday. And I was aware that Sam still needed me to be about.

He was fourteen. Our thing was me taking him to football. To have his dad on the side-line meant a lot to him and to me. He played for Saddleworth 3Ds – a collection of three local villages – on a Sunday morning. Over the last eighteen months they'd developed into a decent side in their division. I loved being there on a Sunday. Nobody had a clue who I was. I would put my hood up. You had to, because it's always freezing. I enjoyed seeing him play and also him knowing his dad was there. To have his game to go to on the Sunday morning would be the ideal decompression from the 5.15 a.m. starts, routines and physical trials of the ultras.

The sense of momentum and people joining our cause was maintained with every step. In the Headingley car park a friend of Stephen Darby's called Dave Cutts pulled his bike out of a car and prepared to join us on the road to Bradford. Dave, who met Stephen through Steve Parkin, his manager at Bradford City, had lost a good friend called Stuart Thackeray, who lasted a year and a half with a very aggressive form of MND. Dave had been a footballer at Boston United and needed cortisone injections in his knees. But that didn't deter him. He just wanted to be on the road with us. 'To be invited to be part of this today, words can't express how proud I am,' Dave said.

Dave's daughter looked after Gemma Middleton, thirty-five, who was diagnosed with MND at twenty-nine. Gemma's face was on an MND awareness poster at railway stations across the country. One afternoon Dave and some friends decided to do the 175-mile coast-to-coast cycle ride. Then he did two triathlons for Gemma Middleton. Like many people who take up causes, he wasn't going to stop.

With Stephen at Valley Parade there was more interaction than there had been with Rob, because Stephen could still converse. But down by the touchline he was visibly upset and overcome with what the team had done. We had a long hug and a chat, again with photographers and camera crews close to it all – immensely challenging for anyone with a serious illness with visible symptoms.

In six days we had seen Doddie, Rob and Stephen, all at different stages of their journey, each with a diagnosis made at separate times. The illness had affected all three in different ways, with no apparent pattern, except that in all three cases there would be changes each time you saw them. I was always looking for those alterations, always trying to calculate where they were on the scale of illness.

For Stephen, perhaps the reception at Valley Parade and the huge local interest made it easier subsequently for him to deal with public appearances. Privately, he was already in touch with Doddie, Rob and Ed. I hope the Valley Parade experience helped him cope better with the spotlight. For people to understand the disease it usually takes people with high profiles to show just what it entails. Stephen had every right of course to keep that private.

I did tease the Bradford folk watching from the main stand with a joke or two. In the late 1990s when the Bulls were in their heyday the Leeds–Bradford rivalry was spicy. The two tribes would still score points off each other when they could. We played a cup game there when Odsal Stadium was being redeveloped – a Challenge Cup fifth round – and one of their assistant coaches came out during the build-up and said he had no doubt they'd remain unbeaten all year. We beat them – away from home. I retold that story to the group on the run into town.

But my word, day 6 was intense. It reminded me of day 5 of the Seven in Seven, when we came to Leeds to see Rob. I remember going home that night and Jayne saying, 'You look shattered.' I went to bed back in Leeds after seeing Rob and Stephen hoping the final ultra wouldn't take me to the dark and painful place the sixth conventional marathon had. I wanted the final leg to Old Trafford to feel celebratory rather than hellish. But there was no doubt as day 7 approached that we'd finish it. Once again, I'd have crawled if I'd had to.

The emotion had continued to pile up. Families were coming out and releasing feelings they'd perhaps suppressed for years or even decades. Some were trying to work their way through grief. Many had been mourning for years and years and were suddenly feeling: I can let go of some of this and feel some kind of release.

Members of our team listened, and at times almost counselled the witnesses to these tragedies. What those people didn't know was that when we set off running again we were still talking about their stories. We took them with us, down the next road, into the following village or town. We shared them with one another. And they're with us still.

I couldn't count the number of people we ran past who welled up and showed us how they felt. That affects you. It affected all of us to see people physically moved, sometimes for reasons we would never know in detail, but in ways we understood from all our time on the journey.

That night back at Headingley Lodge, while my legs were in the compression bags, Rob came up on my TV screen in an interview on *ITV News*. I heard him say through his Eye Gaze: 'I've been in touch with Kevin every day via text. I know that Kev might be in torture, and only say his legs are hurting a bit, but like taking a kick to win us games in the last minute, he will never show weakness, he will die before failing. I just don't want him to injure himself.'

The interviewer reminded Rob that Geoff, his dad, had told me I'd done enough. 'I agree with my dad, he has done enough for everyone, for MND,' said Rob, as I lay on my hotel bed, remote control in hand. 'I'm not surprised at the money he has raised because he is a beacon of hope for everyone who has their own problems. Once he has made up his mind he will see it through.'

The conversation turned to the Rob Burrow Centre for MND, and Rob said: 'I did not set out to have a building named after me, but I had such great feedback for sharing my story and opening up about the disease. I've got something for my kids to remember me by.'

In the *Ultra 7 in 7* documentary made by Ram Films, Dr Agam Jung, the consultant neurologist and director of the Leeds Regional Motor Neurone Disease Centre, said: 'In [the] care delivery model the patient is at the centre. And that is what the Rob Burrow Centre will do. When they come in they will have a peaceful environment: large windows, lots of greenery, not in a cold clinical manner.'

Also featured in the film was the remarkable Ian Flatt, who went up Snowdon in his wheelchair to raise funds for MND care, and who visited us on the ultras. Ian said in the documentary: 'We've got families going to three, four, five different hospitals and clinics across the region. I go to one for my ventilation, I go to a different one for blood tests, I go to a different one to see somebody else. You need to be able to do that in a place of hope.'

In the TV interview I was listening to on my bed, Rob said he had 'stabilised' over the past year but was unable to walk and needed to be carried up and down stairs by Lindsey. He'd had a chest infection. But, he said, 'I feel great on the inside.'

When the interviewer asked about 'difficult conversations' ahead for the pair of them, Lindsey answered: 'We're determined to make as many happy memories and stay as positive as we can. Everything that's been going on and the money that's been raised for MND is something to smile about.'

22

GOING HOME

Day 7 – Bradford City FC to Old Trafford (19 November)

Not everything goes to plan on a seven-day endurance event. It didn't for *BBC Breakfast* when they went over to their live 'Kev Cam' at 8.13 a.m. up a hill between Bradford and Halifax. There we were, running along as normal, until a couple of us veered off to answer the call of nature under a bridge, with the cameras showing it live. Cut to the BBC studio and the two presenters writhing and laughing on their sofa.

Bradford, Halifax, Saddleworth. Hard going, it was, until the hills of home looked kindly on us, and we found ourselves in the Rams Head Inn, Denshaw, with its spectacular view of Oldham and Manchester below and beyond. The Rams Head is a high, 450-year-old shrine for the locals in my area. And it was a lovely haven for us and our families to make the day's first big stop, 32km into our run to the Rugby League World Cup final.

I still can't believe the road over Saddleworth was dry that day. I've driven over that summit maybe 10,000 times going to Leeds and back. This was the only day I'd known it to be still, with no rain. It was like the first day of the Ultra 7 in 7, in Scotland, with its blue skies and gentle breeze.

It was my wish that we didn't run too close to our homes in case it distracted us. Instead, our homes came up the hill to us, cramming into the car park and packing the old stone walls of the pub with loved ones. My mum, dad and sister were there. So were both my brothers-in-law: Steph's husband James and Jayne's older brother Andrew. Also my niece and nephew, uncle and auntie and some cousins. Soon they were joined by another local lad, Paul Scholes, who ducked through the door and into the bar, ready to run with us south-west down into Oldham.

For Scholesy to come, and for us to meet Marcus Stewart, the former footballer who was diagnosed with MND in September 2022, added to the whole experience. I didn't know Marcus lived near us. He came into the Rams Head to connect with Scholesy and the team and was the one banging the MND drum when we left the pub for Denshaw and Grains Bar, passing the hill where Sam played his Sunday morning football.

Scholesy's presence on the run helped show a few more

people what a genuinely nice guy he is. Not enough people see that side of him. I've asked him as a friend to do three things since we both stopped playing and on each occasion he said yes straight away – never with any conditions. Each time it was: 'Yes, where do you want me, what do you need?'

To see him with a collection bucket was striking and reinforced the message that we were all in this together. In the pub in my village, long after the Ultra 7 in 7, David walked in to see Scholesy having a pint. When Paul walked over to David all he wanted to talk about was the run. He was David's hero, so you can imagine how a lifelong Man Utd fan felt having Scholesy wanting to talk to him in a pub about the run they had both been on.

Back on the run, home was tantalisingly close, but we still had work to do, a finishing line to cross, an appointment to keep at Old Trafford. We freewheeled down through Moorside, to the area where I'd taken up rugby as a boy, to Watersheddings. More and more people flooded on to the pavements, the reception growing ever more boisterous and supportive. It was like running through a movie.

As we descended, I ducked off at Watersheddings to give Shane Wilson's widow Karen a cuddle. All the kids and junior sections from my old amateur club Waterhead were also out, along with guys who had helped me through my career. And a bit further on was my brother Ian, who I ran across the road to hug. Also there were my sister-in-law

Vicky and father-in-law Peter. Throughout the week we had soaked up the emotions of people we met. Then, to see people who meant so much to us, when we were absolutely shattered, sent us into overload.

Running through Oldham was beautiful. We had purposely avoided coming through the Saddleworth villages where many of us lived because it would save us three miles not to. Plus, I didn't want to run past my house. But I couldn't have asked for a better welcome home from the area I've always lived in.

At the bottom of the hill, Scholesy said his goodbyes and veered off left, leaving the team to reflect on what a joy it had been to run with one of the great English footballers. Up ahead was a Morrisons in Failsworth where soup and piles of sandwiches had been laid on for us, and more people with MND and their families came to speak to us in the supermarket.

Central Manchester was only 6km away. The music blared, the jokes kept coming, the end was in sight. Now we were running through the Metropolis for a brief stop at an MND event in Deansgate, before the final leg, out towards the big spaceship of Old Trafford, where Samoa and Australia were about to square up. The team's vehicles fought their way through Manchester's complicated traffic system so we could keep the whole operation running right to the end – to Hotel Football, where we were cheered into the lobby, to gather our senses in the top-floor bar.

Through the windows of their high function suite we gazed across to the stadium where I'd played so many Grand Finals. Exhausted but euphoric, the team buzzed around and took refreshments as we awaited our call to cross the road and make our way to the tunnel outside the dressing rooms.

But first I called the team together and told them: 'What we've done this week, you might never, ever do anything like this for the rest of your life. But what I will say to you is that you'll remember it for the rest of your life. And every time you see each person in this room, now, wherever we are, you'll have an unbelievable bond, and you'll know we've done something special together. We've helped a lot of people. I know I started the week by saying I hope you have the best week of your life. I can stand here and say – I have, I hope you guys have too.'

When I said 'best week of my life', context, of course, was everything. I didn't mean to elevate it above the most precious family moments – me and Jayne being married, the boys being born and so on. I meant the best week of my life outside of family events.

Phil Daly called us together to leave the hotel.

'I was told we had time for a pint,' Martin objected.

'Not by me you weren't,' said Phil.

And down we all went in the lifts and across to the stadium to mingle in the Old Trafford tunnel while the first half of the game played out in front of us – a comfortable final, as it turned out, for Australia, whose coach, Mal Meninga, later came over to say hello.

Then it was our turn. I wanted the whole Ultra 7 in 7 team on the pitch. We emerged from the tunnel into the neon glow, the Stretford End to our left, the crowd applauding, and Sally Nugent visible, with a microphone, in the centre circle.

I made my way across the grass to join her, the noise rising in the stadium.

This is what I said: 'That team is incredible. I think you all know why: Rob Burrow, Doddie Weir, Stephen Darby, Ed Slater, the full MND community. The full rugby league community have got behind the MND community. I can't thank you enough.'

Sally: 'Kevin, you have done seven ultra-marathons in seven days. You said you were just going for a run for a mate. What kept you going?'

Me: 'That exact thought. It's all about friendship . . . and the love for Rob.'

Another surge of feeling went round Old Trafford. I paused to collect my thoughts.

'I know that everyone feels the same way that I do about Rob Burrow. He's an absolute champion. The way the Burrow family have been so courageous and brave, we just wanted to be a great friend. And if we can all try and be a bit of a better friend from time to time, I think we'll have a better place to live in.'

Another wave of applause, another pause.

Sally read out the total raised to that point: £1.3 million (over the coming weeks it would rise to £2.7 million). Then she asked: 'What's your message to the people who supported you?'

'It's just a massive thank you,' I replied. 'We met some incredible people along the journey from Edinburgh, but there's one thing for sure – that our country cares. It cares about people who need help. And the MND community need us, they need support, they need love, and we've got to find a cure.'

We left the pitch. The game resumed. Australia were crowned world champions – again.

It was time for our own team celebration.

I was desperate for a shower and disappeared to have one. I felt brand new, elated, happy to be going home. One by one the team went back to their everyday lives. Each will have sifted their memories of the week. One of the first messages I received was a lovely letter from Sally Light, the CEO of the MND Association, who wrote: 'As you have said so clearly, it has given hope to the MND community and shown them that people care. Heartfelt thanks from all of us to you and the brilliant team around you.'

The MND Association were the beacon, and I appreciated the chance to reflect in an interview for their *MND Matters* podcast, where I said: 'The biggest thing you can give people is hope, and I like to think we provided some more, through the funds that have been generated and the awareness that's been created.

'All those that came and stood at the roadside in the rain, all those who nipped out in their pyjamas for those early morning stints, and brought some energy for us, brought some smiles . . .

'We met so many wonderful families . . . it's you people who made it really special for us. We loved every single minute of representing the MND community, and we'd do it all again in a heartbeat.'

I slept really well that night. Part of me had been unsure that we'd actually be able to finish it. When I reviewed the week I asked whether there was anything we could have done differently. Answer: nothing of any significance. The week had gone mostly as planned. The following morning, despite having the chance to sleep in, I was awake early, true to the ultras routine of being up before dawn and ready to run.

I opened my laptop and worked, which felt bizarre: back to earth with a bang. I was incredibly happy to be home but also missed the routine, missed being out with the team, missed running, even getting ready in the dark before sunrise. But the strongest emotion was relief to be home with Jayne and the boys and pride at having completed it.

Sam's football game was cancelled because of the weather. I lifted some weights and turned my legs over on the bike. That night we went out as a family for a meal. That was lovely. Then on the Monday we went to do *BBC Break-fast*, and I was back with the team again. Everyone was buzzing – do you remember this, do you remember that?

Physically, though, I was run down. At the Leicester coaches meeting on the Tuesday I can remember my eyes stinging with tiredness. Fatigue had finally caught up with me.

23

FAREWELL TO DODDIE

The way I heard the news was eerie. We'd finished the Ultra 7 in 7 at 4.05 p.m. the previous Saturday. Seven days later at 4.05 p.m., in honour of us reaching the finish line, I began running for thirty minutes on the treadmill in our garage. The second I stepped off, some awful words landed on my phone.

The message was from Doddie's old team-mate Hoggy – Carl Hogg – to say Doddie had passed away, at fifty-two, with Kathy and his family by his side. It was tough to absorb on every level. Right away I called out for Jayne and she came into the garage asking what was up. She could see the state I was in. I couldn't take it in that Doddie had left us just thirteen days after we had seen him at Murrayfield. Plainly he hadn't been well that day.

Now I was in our garage, distraught, reflecting on the enormity of him turning up to see us off on the run. My final image of him – as it was for everyone – was him with his sons on the pitch before the Scotland–All Blacks game later that day.

And then, as I tried to deal with the shock, my thoughts turned to Rob, and what the news might do to him. I messaged Lindsey straight away, then left it a while before making direct contact with Rob. My plan before Doddie's death had been to see Rob on the Thursday but I very quickly changed that to the Monday.

Inevitably I travelled over to see him with concerns bouncing around my mind. I needn't have worried quite so much. Lindsey had told me in a message that Rob had been profoundly upset. But in my note to Rob I told him that Doddie would have wanted us to carry on, and I said we would, without fail. When I arrived, Rob reflected that message back to me. I saw him take strength from the idea that we'd carry on in Doddie's honour.

Doddie had left a huge mark on Rob. On one level his death gave Rob an even greater urge to fight, however swamped he felt by sadness at losing his friend. After I saw him that Monday I was less worried about him because he seemed more determined than ever to continue helping others with the disease.

It was a longer visit than usual. And once we'd settled our hearts down from the news about Doddie, I tried another way of keeping his spirits up. I ripped into him on a couple of bits I always teased him about: the fact that he used to go on the sunbed, and the fact that he was the only rugby player

I knew who travelled to away games with hair straighteners in his bag. I hammered him. Odd though it may sound, it always had him laughing. Then I hugged him again and left.

Rob's tweet about Doddie's death conveyed both his grief and his anger at the government delays in handing over the £50 million it had promised in November 2021 to help find a cure. Rob was very hot on that topic. Soon there would be a shift in the government's handling of the money. But before the authorities got a move on, Rob gave it to them straight: 'So sad to hear the news of the passing of my MND hero Doddie Weir. I'm sorry to say, how many more warriors die before this stupid government give the 50m they said they would give. I'm absolutely gutted to see my friendly giraffe die. You are the reason for being so positive. RIP.'

Earlier Rob had said on *BBC Breakfast*: 'I've heard it is curable but underfunded in the past; with the money supposedly coming from the government, the money Kev has raised, over £6 million, would start it off. But this Tory government has blood on their hands because it kills six people every day.'

At the same time I told the BBC: 'I understand that with anything like this there is an element of red tape, but then I look at some of the other ways they have spent money and I don't think they have been scrutinised in the same way this has. That's what I don't understand, and [what] disappoints me, because there are people dying and families are being ravaged and being left.

'The most important thing for someone who has been diagnosed is time, and they're running out of time. I can't see any excuse or reason why that money has been held back.'

It was Boris Johnson who in November 2021 had announced the £50 million pledge to help find a cure for MND. The then Prime Minister said it would 'transform the fight' against the disease. But for the next year the money was tied up in bureaucracy. On 12 December 2022 – after Doddie's death, Rob's comments and the Ultra 7 in 7 – the government succumbed to public pressure. On that day the Health Secretary Steve Barclay said he would 'slash red tape' to release funding to biomedical research centres. 'I'm grateful to the United to End MND campaign for their work raising awareness,' he said, 'and I warmly congratulate Kevin Sinfield on his epic achievement completing seven ultra-marathons, as well as remembering the late Doddie Weir for his outstanding contribution over the past five years.'

We didn't want credit. We just wanted the money to go where it was needed. In their own words the government were now promising, without precise dates:

- £29.5 million of government funding to be invested immediately through specialist research centres and partnerships with leading researchers
- a further £20.5 million to accelerate work on the most promising treatments through open call processes

Events were moving fast. The Health Secretary spoke six days after Eddie Jones had been sacked as England's rugby union head coach, a week before Doddie's memorial service and nine days ahead of a special night for Rob at the BBC *Sports Personality of the Year* show. By the time Doddie's service came round, I'd left Leicester Tigers for a new job. I'll say more about that in the following chapter.

I probably needed that day in my car on the way to the funeral to reflect on Doddie and my time with him. I played Dire Straits' *Brothers in Arms* several times as I drove up though the Borders, not recognising too many of the places we had run through until I pulled into Melrose and met Hoggy, who went above and beyond to make me feel comfortable around people I didn't really know. He met me at the church and sat with me for the service.

At Melrose Parish Church, Doddie's sons, Hamish, Angus and Ben, wore tartan suits like the ones their father loved. They recited 'Requiem for Doddie (The Mad Giraffe)', a poem by Timmy Douglas. The Scottish Rugby Union live-streamed the service on their website and around 1,000 people packed the stands of the Melrose ground to listen to an audio feed. At the start of the service, the organist played 'Going Home', the tune from *Local Hero*.

Hoggy spoke beautifully about Doddie. Wonderful words. He did him proud. Rob Wainwright and John Jeffrey, fellow ex-Scotland internationals, also spoke superbly. I was slightly starstruck to meet Gavin Hastings, the great

Scotland full-back, and was glad to catch up with Gary Armstrong, the former scrum-half, who sat behind me in the church.

Hoggy recited Doddie's motto: 'Enjoy life while you can – you just don't know what's round the corner.'

Over the preceding eighteen months or so I'd picked up precisely that message from Rob: enjoy life while you have the chance. He never said it explicitly, but I know it was in his mind. A big part of how I viewed my own life was the inspiration provided by Rob not to accept being unhappy.

By the time we walked out of the church, Steve Borthwick had been unveiled as the new England head coach, and it was known that I would be the new defence coach.

I stayed in Melrose for a couple of hours, left just after 4 p.m., and drove to Cleator Moor in Cumbria, famous for its mines and railways, to run with Gary McKee, who was on a mission to complete a marathon on all 365 days of 2022, to raise at least £1 million for charity. He did it, too, wrapping up marathon no. 365 on New Year's Eve, at the end of 9,563 miles.

In a hotel in deepest darkest Cleator Moor I sat eating alone, reflecting on a tumultuous day, until Gary arrived and joined me for a drink at the bar. The following morning we ran.

Steve Borthwick had been keen for me to attend Doddie's memorial service. But I'd also felt I ought to get his approval to run a marathon 'up there' the next day.

'Up where?' Steve asked.

'Cumbria,' I said.

Yes, said Steve, straight away.

Steve's from Carlisle. A proud Cumbrian himself, he was bound to say yes.

One final outing before Christmas was approaching: the BBC's *Sports Personality of the Year*, where Rob received the Helen Rollason Award and I was given a special one conceived to go with Rob's. I didn't need an award. I was just so happy for Rob, and it was pleasing that the majority of the Ultra 7 in 7 team were back together again.

I always find that, since he lost his voice, if I have to speak publicly with Rob alongside me I get emotional. At *SPOTY* I was incredibly nervous. I didn't want to cry in front of people again, didn't want to get emotional on live TV. Had I spoken first I'd have been fine. But instead Rob talked first, through his Eye Gaze. Then the BBC played a video of him. It took me right back to the toughest emotions, which made speaking hard. You're trying to get across clearly to the audience and the viewers at home why the fund-raising is so important to the people on stage with you and the wider MND community, while your feelings are overwhelming you.

I had an idea what I wanted to say, but no script. The car to take us to *SPOTY* was late. Everyone was already sitting down and there was no time to rehearse. I hit the topics I wanted to but they didn't come out as I'd planned because

I was so emotional. At Old Trafford after the Ultra 7 in 7 I'd talked about people in our country caring, and how powerful sport can be. I wanted to return to those themes. So I said: 'From the start this has been a big team effort. Everyone has got behind what we've tried to do. Rob is probably the most inspirational bloke in the UK. He has inspired us to be better friends. In sport and certainly in rugby, the connections you make, the friends, don't just stop when the whistle goes.

'Sport is powerful enough to bring communities together. What we have witnessed is a nation that cares about the MND community.'

Straight after the show we went in to film a piece for *BBC Breakfast* for the following morning. I had a lovely moment with Ed Slater when we were able to hand him a cheque from the Ultra 7 in 7, which he put in his top pocket. Happy Christmas, Ed.

And as we walked through I bumped into Barrie McDermott and Keith Senior, two great Leeds Rhinos team-mates. They both said: I don't know how on earth, when your bottom lip's going during a speech, you're able to bring it back.

I told them: all I'm trying to do is fight against crying.

24

NEXT STOP TWICKENHAM

By the time I left home to head to Melrose for Doddie's funeral I knew Leicester Tigers had released me to become England rugby union defence coach. My sadness at leaving a club I loved working at was mixed with a sense of pride and adventure.

The Six Nations Championship would start on Saturday 4 February 2023. Our first opponents, at Twickenham, would be the country I had driven north to for the farewell to Doddie. Many of its greatest players had been there to pay their respects. You won't be surprised to hear that one or two of them had been keen to know what might happen now with England.

The gist of it was that Steve was invited by the Rugby Football Union to take over from Eddie Jones, who lost the job in the first week of December. And Steve wanted me in his coaching set-up. For all that to happen, the RFU had to agree terms with Leicester for our release.

It was resolved on Saturday 17 December, the day of our 23–16 win over Clermont Auvergne in the Heineken Champions Cup, after which Steve announced to the players and staff that he was taking the England job. When he'd finished, I made a similar announcement.

I think everyone had expected Steve to be going but were less sure I would be leaving Leicester at the same time. For a while it was unclear whether I'd be staying on for a period to help Richard Wigglesworth bed in as Steve's replacement. The process was stressful. On the Friday night Jayne took a picture of me with my head in my hands. 'Even when you left Leeds I never saw you like this with your head in your hands,' she said.

Over the previous sixteen months I'd built some incredible relationships with staff and players and derived huge fulfilment from working at Leicester. I was so grateful for my time with them all. And I've always been conscious that it's difficult for a coach to leave a team midway through a season when it's of his own accord. I struggled with that. I spoke to Steve about perhaps staying at Leicester until the end of the season but that wasn't an option from the England end of it. I understood that fully.

Once I'd examined all the elements I felt you couldn't put a price on being involved with a national team with a World Cup approaching. The opportunity was too good to turn down. On that Saturday after the Clermont game I wasn't sure whether that was my last game or I'd be around for a few more weeks. But the decision was made that the players would be told straight after that game. I hadn't prepared anything. Steve announced to the lads that he was stepping down and it was my turn next, in a packed changing room. All the rugby staff and players were in there.

The fact that I moved on didn't mean the friendships I'd formed would fade. After I said my bit on that Saturday evening I was in touch with pretty much everyone in that room via text or phone. There wasn't one player I didn't enjoy working with, not a single member of staff who wasn't patient or giving with me.

In that coaching team I don't think I could have had a better group of people around me: Aled Walters, Brett Deacon, Matt Egan, Wiggy, Matt Smith, Luc Thomas, our other analyst, and Tom Harrison. An unbelievable coaching team. The room was so tight and close. They understood what a fabulous opportunity it was for me. But it was hard to say goodbye.

The following day, Sunday 18 December, back home, was extremely strange. I'd prepped for us to play Gloucester the following week. I kept opening my laptop, then closing it. Opening it, and closing it again. I was a bit lost because I'd had all this direction and had worked incredibly hard and now didn't know what to do. My new job hadn't started yet. I was in that middle ground.

I started thinking about the England job on the drive up to Melrose on the Monday. I was trying to grasp what were the big issues we needed to go after. Steve would be busy with a long list of tasks so I needed to get on and be productive while he sorted the big priorities.

My first job was to watch the weekend's games. Reality struck home when my new kit arrived between Christmas and New Year, with the red rose on. I'd never worn that before. That week I started putting things together. My targets were to go through the autumn internationals, speak to analysts, ring some of the senior boys, look for big wins early, build relationships, explain what we wanted. With the commute to Leicester gone, I was able to remove the 4.23 a.m. daily alarm call from my clock.

In the first days of the new year forty-five England players assembled in Liverpool and Gloucester to undergo a battery of tests. It gave us an ideal opportunity to meet the players. And at the University of Gloucestershire's Oxstalls campus I did a long session with the press. I told them I'd seen a 'glint and sparkle in the players' eyes' and talked about how Rob had influenced this new direction in my career.

'Rob's inspired me in so many different ways and it's probably a large reason why I'm here,' I said. 'My old mate got diagnosed with motor neurone disease back in December 2019. Without that horrible news I'm not sure I would have come down this path. Towards the back end of 2020 I was able to do the first challenge and as soon as I finished it I knew I had to do something different with my life. A lot of that is based around Rob. He's faced with this horrific disease and I realised I needed to take some risk and find more challenge in my life.'

In thirty-two days we'd be playing Scotland at Twickenham. Doddie's clan would be heading south to confront us. In no sport can people be friend and foe at the same time like they can in rugby.

POSTSCRIPT

What I learned over the first three challenges is that running is moving fast enough to hit many locations and have interactions with a large number of people. You're moving slowly enough to make connections, but fast enough to get from A to B in a decent time.

If you walk, those interactions aren't fleeting and you can't cover the same distance from start to finish. If you cycle, those connections don't happen because it's too quick. The speed we run at lends itself to being a great way to bring communities together. They're out to support us and then they're back indoors. It's not like someone's flying past on a bike, or walking, where you might spend too long in one place.

The interactions we've had from running have been so special, so numerous and so varied that I ended the Ultra 7 in 7 feeling we would run again, possibly in 2023. Running is the perfect vehicle. The trilogy I completed in 2022 was probably not going to be the end of it.

At the end of the *Ultra 7 in 7* documentary, I'd said with a smile: 'Of all the Rocky films, my favourite is probably *Rocky IV*.'

The biggest challenge now would be for run no. 4 to be tough enough for BBC *Breakfast* to want to support it, but not so big that people might become sick of us. That's a fine balance, given the number of different diseases and illnesses there are out there – the sheer number of good causes. When is enough enough? Actually, there's no 'enough' – but when is the right time to be less high profile, while still sticking to your task?

We hadn't yet taken on London. After I took the England job I had an image of finishing a challenge one day at Twickenham, and hearing the kind of roar we heard at half-time between Australia and Samoa.

I'd always planned for the Rob Burrow Leeds Marathon to be the legacy piece. Over 10,000 people had signed up for the inaugural race in May 2023.

The whole ethos and slogan behind that new marathon has been 'run for a mate, with a mate'.

That's the sentiment we drew on for the Ultra 7 in 7 – run for a mate.

It doesn't have to be for MND. It could be for different charities, for different reasons, to show how much you care.

Just go the extra mile for a mate.

ACKNOWLEDGEMENTS

Talking of teamwork, it takes many people to produce a book, and I would like to thank those who helped me tell the story of my life.

This autobiography came into being from countless hours of conversations with Paul Hayward, my co-writer. We started outside my childhood home, and carried the discussions all the way through my work with Rob Burrow and the MND community to me leaving Leicester Tigers to join England. It was an intense and sometimes emotional walk back through time. I am delighted to say Paul is now a good friend.

My literary agent Ruth Cairns of Featherstone Cairns teamed up with Ben Brusey, Publishing Director of Penguin Random House, to make it possible. My thanks to Ruth, Ben, and to his colleagues Laurie Ip Fung Chun and Dan Balado, for their work on the manuscript, to Callum Crute for his work on the pictures, to Rebecca Ikin and Hope

Butler on the marketing, to Mat Watterson and his team on sales, to Klara Zak on the publicity and Emma Grey Gelder on the cover. I couldn't be happier with my choice of publisher.

I owe huge gratitude to those who've helped me to this point in sport, life and in our MND work; to all my team-mates and friends across rugby; to Rob and all those working to defeat MND; to the great team we assembled for the three charity challenges; to Sally Nugent, Claire Ryan and Richard Frediani at *BBC Breakfast*, who backed us from the start.

And of course to my family: parents Ray and Beryl, brother Ian and sister Stephanie, and all who have joined us in the Sinfield club.

Finally and most importantly, Jayne, Jack and Sam, my wife and sons, the foundation of my life and my whole world – and this book, which is dedicated to them. I love you very much.

MY CAREER IN NUMBERS

RUGBY LEAGUE

LEEDS RHINOS (1997–2015)

- 1997 – 2 substitute appearances
- 1998 – 2 substitute appearances, 1 try, 4 points
- 1999 – 9 starts (12 sub), 2 tries, 12 goals, 32 points
- 2000 – 19 starts (7 sub), 7 tries, 28 points
- 2001 – 32 starts (1 sub), 10 tries, 29 goals, 1 drop goal, 99 points
- 2002 – 30 starts (2 sub), 8 tries, 32 goals, 96 points
- 2003 – 34 starts (1 sub), 6 tries, 122 goals, 5 drop goals, 273 points
- 2004 – 31 starts, 4 tries, 152 goals, 3 drop goals, 323 points
- 2005 – 31 starts, 6 tries, 149 goals, 2 drop goals, 324 points

- 2006 – 26 starts, 3 tries, 105 goals, 1 drop goal, 223 points
- 2007 – 32 starts, 6 tries, 139 goals, 3 drop goals, 305 points
- 2008 – 34 starts, 4 tries, 137 goals, 3 drop goals, 293 points
- 2009 – 29 starts, 4 tries, 121 goals, 3 drop goals, 261 points
- 2010 – 29 starts, 4 tries, 121 goals, 4 drop goals, 262 points
- 2011 – 36 starts, 2 tries, 160 goals, 2 drop goals, 330 points
- 2012 – 37 starts, 7 tries, 168 goals, 5 drop goals, 369 points
- 2013 – 28 starts, 4 tries, 106 goals, 2 drop goals, 230 points
- 2014 – 27 starts, 5 tries, 102 goals, 2 drop goals, 226 points
- 2015 – 26 starts (4 sub), 3 tries, 137 goals, 3 drop goals, 289 points

LEEDS RHINOS TOTAL

- *521 appearances (490 starts + 31 as substitute), 86 tries, 1,792 goals, 39 drop goals, 3,967 points*

RUGBY LEAGUE (*cont.*)

Great Britain (2001–2003, 2005, 2007)

- 8 starts (7 sub), 2 tries, 18 goals, 44 points, 14 caps

England (2000–2001, 2008–2013)

- 26 starts (3 sub), 5 tries, 100 goals, 220 points, 26 caps

Lancashire (2001–2003)

- 3 starts (1 sub)

RUGBY UNION

YORKSHIRE CARNEGIE (2015–2016)

- 18 starts, 43 goals, 122 points

COACHING CAREER

LEICESTER TIGERS (2021–2022)

- Defence coach – 2021–2022 Premiership Rugby Champions

CAREER TOTAL

- *569 appearances (531 starts + 38 sub), 93 tries, 1,910 goals, 39 drop goals, 4,231 points*

MND FUNDRAISING

- 2020 – Seven in Seven challenge: £2.7 million
  o Seven marathons in seven consecutive days, totalling over 183 miles / 295 km.
- 2021 – The Extra Mile challenge: £2 million+
  o 101 miles in 24 hours, from Welford Road to Headingley stadium.
- 2022 – Ultra 7 in 7 challenge: over £2.5 million (at time of writing)
  o 7 back-to-back ultra-marathons (over 40 miles or 60 km a day, totalling over 280 miles/420 km), running from Edinburgh to Manchester via Melrose, Newcastle, Middlesbrough, York, Leeds and Bradford.

FUNDRAISING TOTAL: £7 MILLION+

HONOURS

- Grand Final winner x 7

- Grand Final runner-up x 1
- Challenge Cup winner x 2
- Challenge Cup runner-up x 5
- World Club Challenge winner x 3
- World Club Challenge runner-up x 3
- League Leaders' Shield winner x 3
- Leeds Rhinos and Super League records for most goals and points
- Super League record for most appearances
- Third most appearances for Leeds
- Third-highest rugby league points scorer
- England's highest points scorer
- 2005 World Club Challenge man of the match
- 2005 Lance Todd Trophy winner
- 2009 and 2012 Harry Sunderland award winner
- 2012 Golden Boot
- 2014 MBE
- 2015 Sports Personality of the Year runner-up
- 2017 Coached England to the Rugby League World Cup Final
- 2021 OBE
- 2021–2022 Premiership Champions
- 2022 Sports Personality of the Year Special Award
- 2023 Appointed England rugby union defence coach

ILLUSTRATION CREDITS

Plate Section 1

p. 1 Both images: Author's collection

p. 2 Both images: Author's collection

p. 3 Both images: Author's collection

p. 4 Top: © Leeds Rhinos. Bottom: © PA Images / Alamy Stock Photo

p. 5 Top: © Jamie McDonald / Getty. Bottom: © Jamie McDonald / Getty

p. 6 Top: Author's collection. Bottom: © Getty

p. 7 Top and bottom left: Author's collection. Right: © Clive Brunskill / Getty

p. 8 Top: © Daniel L. Smith / Stringer / Getty. Bottom: © Clive Brunskill / Getty

Plate Section 2

p. 1 Top: © Sportsfile / Getty. Bottom left: © PA Images / Alamy Stock Photo. Bottom right: © Paul Ellis / PA Images / Alamy Stock Photo

p. 2 Top: © David Rogers / Getty. Bottom: © David Rogers / Getty

p. 3 Top: © Reuters / Alamy Stock Photo. Bottom: © PA Images / Alamy Stock Photo

p. 4 Top left: © Becca Wright / Penguin Random House UK. All other images: © Paul Hayward

p. 5 Top: © PA Images / Alamy Stock Photo. Bottom: © Carol Ste / Alamy Stock Photo

p. 6 Top: © Naomi Baker / Getty. Bottom: © Lewis Storey / Stringer / Getty

p. 7 Top: © PA Images / Alamy Stock Photo. Middle: © Leeds Rhinos. Bottom: PA Images / Alamy Stock Photo

p. 8 Both images: © Paul Hayward

INDEX

297

World Cup, Rugby League
(1972) 255
(2000) 74, 79
(2008) 79
(2013) 79, 80
(2017) 97
(2022) 1, 4, 197, 207, 218–19,
264, 266, 286
World Cup, Rugby Union
(2003) 54, 82
(2007) 83
(2019) 133
(2023) 6, 281–2

Wynyard Estate 241

York Minster 247–8, 254
Yorkshire 26, 38, 58, 70, 115, 156,
160, 182, 184, 186, 192,
212, 215
Yorkshire County Cricket Club
115
Yorkshire Marathon 182, 186–7,
212
'You'll Never Walk Alone' 238
Your Housing Group
(YHG) 214